Advance Praise for *Asperger's from the Inside Out*

"Refreshing, concise, systematic, and to the point. It spans the history of ASD diagnosis, the identity crises involved in diagnosis. . . . It explores positive versus negative takes on ASD and their consequences, the resonating impact of a diagnosis on other family members, but, more so, gives spiritual guidance about more or less healthy ways of managing all these things and the consequences that choices have for each individual. Beautifully alive with quotes from a broad range of voices with ASD, this is a helpful addition to the world of autism-related literature."

—Donna Williams, author of
Nobody Nowhere and *The Jumbled Jigsaw*

"Michael John Carley is an articulate and passionate advocate for people with Asperger's syndrome. His engaging book offers a thoughtful and creative roadmap for people with Asperger's and their loved ones."

—Mark Roithmayr, President, Autism Speaks

"Michael Carley is unique in his ability to combine and integrate his experiences with conclusions and insights that are remarkable and powerful. His unique ability to integrate, conceptualize, compare, and contrast at such a high level is what makes his work stand out."

—Gary Mesibov, Ph.D., Director, Division TEACCH,
Professor of Psychology and Psychiatry at the
University of North Carolina at Chapel Hill

"A wonderfully candid and encouraging book about navigating the world of Asperger's syndrome. I recommend it to everyone, on or off the spectrum, who believes in creating a more tolerant and inclusive society."

—Sigourney Weaver, actress

"Michael John Carley is not only a successful leader in the AS community, he has proven himself to be a gifted writer. *Everyone* who is involved with the Asperger's syndrome community, their family, friends, and the professionals who help them *must* read this book!"

—Susan J. Moreno, M.A., A.B.S., President,
MAAP Services for Autism and Asperger Syndrome

continued . . .

D0063915

Asperger's
from the
Inside Out

*A Supportive and Practical Guide for
Anyone with Asperger's Syndrome*

MICHAEL JOHN CARLEY

Executive Director, GRASP
The Global and Regional Asperger Syndrome Partnership

Foreword by Peter F. Gerhardt, Ed.D.
President, Organization for Autism Research

A Perigee Book

A PERIGEE BOOK
Published by the Penguin Group
Penguin Group (USA) Inc.
375 Hudson Street, New York, New York 10014, USA
Penguin Group (Canada), 90 Eglinton Avenue East, Suite 700, Toronto, Ontario M4P 2Y3, Canada (a division of Pearson Penguin Canada Inc.) ● Penguin Books Ltd., 80 Strand, London WC2R 0RL, England ● Penguin Group Ireland, 25 St. Stephen's Green, Dublin 2, Ireland (a division of Penguin Books Ltd.) ● Penguin Group (Australia), 250 Camberwell Road, Camberwell, Victoria 3124, Australia (a division of Pearson Australia Group Pty. Ltd.) ● Penguin Books India Pvt. Ltd., 11 Community Centre, Panchsheel Park, New Delhi—110 017, India ● Penguin Group (NZ), 67 Apollo Drive, Rosedale, North Shore 0632, New Zealand (a division of Pearson New Zealand Ltd.) ● Penguin Books (South Africa) (Pty.) Ltd., 24 Sturdee Avenue, Rosebank, Johannesburg 2196, South Africa

Penguin Books Ltd., Registered Offices: 80 Strand, London WC2R 0RL, England

While the author has made every effort to provide accurate telephone numbers and Internet addresses at the time of publication, neither the publisher nor the author assumes any responsibility for errors, or for changes that occur after publication. Further, the publisher does not have any control over and does not assume any responsibility for author or third-party websites or their content.

Copyright © 2008 by Michael John Carley
Cover photograph by Ron Haviv / VII
Cover design by Charles Bjorklund
Text design by Tiffany Estreicher

First edition: April 2008

Library of Congress Cataloging-in-Publication Data

Carley, Michael John.
   Asperger's from the inside out : a supportive and practical guide for anyone with Asperger's syndrome / Michael John Carley ; foreword by Peter F. Gerhardt.— 1st ed.
     p.   cm.
   ISBN-13: 978-0-399-53397-6
   1. Asperger's syndrome—Popular works.   I. Title.
   RC553.A88C37   2008
   616.85'8832—dc22   2007045438

PRINTED IN THE UNITED STATES OF AMERICA

10 9 8 7 6 5 4 3 2 1

PUBLISHER'S NOTE: Neither the publisher nor the author is engaged in rendering professional advice or services to the individual reader. The ideas, procedures, and suggestions contained in this book are not intended as a substitute for consulting with your physician. All matters regarding your health require medical supervision. Neither the author nor the publisher shall be liable or responsible for any loss or damage allegedly arising from any information or suggestion in this book.

Most Perigee books are available at special quantity discounts for bulk purchases for sales promotions, premiums, fund-raising, or educational use. Special books, or book excerpts, can also be created to fit specific needs. For details, write: Special Markets, Penguin Group (USA) Inc., 375 Hudson Street, New York, New York 10014.

For Grandpa Chet,
These pages contain perhaps the only words he didn't have.
My shelter,
as well as my challenge.

And for Kathryn,
who rebuilt the world.

Acknowledgments

ALMOST all the roads to this book pass through GRASP. So first and foremost thanks to my Board of Directors for providing me with a job that reflects more credit on me than I deserve: Liane Holliday Willey, Ed.D.; David Kowalski; Michael McManmon, Ed.D.; Valerie Paradiz, Ph.D.; and David Tobis, Ph.D. Past Board member Dr. Peter Gerhardt also deserves much credit for GRASP's formation and early development.

Thanks also to those at the Fund for Social Change, especially Dr. Tobis and Mr. John Courtney, for start-up funding, and also for a fellowship prior to starting GRASP that turned a fund-raising neophyte into a fund-raiser, albeit one who still has much to learn. Continued thanks to them for affordable rent, friendship, and the comfort of sharing workspace with people I admire.

Thanks to all those early compatriots in the 2001–2002 Manhattan support group whence GRASP began, especially Karl Wittig, Allen Markman, Michael Madore, and especially Philip Snyder-Jimenez; for dreaming big when I thought such lofty ideas didn't have a prayer.

Thanks also to our part-time and per-project employees, especially Oya Erez, and Ben Fox, who do nothing but reward our faith in them.

Thanks to all the organizations GRASP has partnered with, and the special people that run them, most especially my most endurable friend, Pat Schissel. These folks continuously show that collaborative behavior in nonprofits serves everyone.

Thanks to brilliant clinicians and friends like Dr. Lynda Geller, Dr. Valerie Gaus, Dr. Shana Nichols, Dr. Gerhardt, and Dr. Brenda Smith-Myles, who give me somewhere to turn when my lack of a doctorate leaves me scratching my head.

Thanks to all of GRASP's volunteers and past Benefit Committee members for helping make our honorees feel as honored as we wanted.

Thanks to all those like Sue Moreno, of MAAP Services, Inc., and the countless others who made a commitment through their organizations to have the voices of people on the spectrum heard—back when doing so was a significant risk to their credibility. All of the above were responsible for believing in GRASP at our earliest and vulnerable stages. Their word of mouth, coupled with our efforts, put forth an air of credibility when we needed one most.

To all those who have supported GRASP where it has kept us alive—through funding—huge thanks. No matter how good the program content is for any organization, unless it is sustained, it dies; or worse, falls into disrespect for failing to keep itself afloat. In addition to the countless donors GRASP has been blessed with, hearty thanks go to those foundations who have been brave enough to support us when others were reluctant to acknowledge peer-run supports: This includes the Fund for Social Change, the IDT Telephone Corporation Foundation, the Hamilton Family Foundation, the Bell Family Foundation, the van Ameringen Foundation, the Charles and Mildred Schnurmacher Foundation, and the Simons Family Foundation. Thanks also to those who have given to GRASP in other areas, such as the legal counsel of Stroock, Stroock & Lavan; the web services of CounterIntuity; the web marketing services of Online Search Solutions; the many churches, synagogues, and libraries that provide free meeting space for our networks; and the many universities, conferences, hospitals, schools, and larger autism organizations that have brought us in to speak.

Large thanks go out to all those GRASP members who have gone through this diagnostic process, and then shared the experience. My having heard the multitude of stories from these brave pioneers has not just given the authority to this book, but it has also set a tone for others—the many others—who will go through the process in the future.

The largest thanks, however, go to those who are GRASP's strongest engine, our regional facilitators—people on the spectrum who voluntarily cater to their communities, running networks, who together affirmed that GRASP was an organization whose time had come. They are Julie Bundrick, Cathy Collins, Rebecca Gbasha, Kathy Grant, Robert E. Hedin, Tom Jacobs, Brian King, Steve Lawson, April Malone, Brandon Plank, Trista J. Rupp Plott, Joel Spector, Laura Wysolmierski, and those who may have sprung up since the writing of this book.

Thanks to a generous and supportive editor, Marian Lizzi; and special thanks to a great advisor, patient professional, and friend: my agent, Susan Ramer, of Don Congdon Associates.

Thanks to my wife *and* love of my life, Kathryn, who typed up *so* many notes for me. And lastly, thanks to my boys, who in fatherhood give me the best job in the world. Every decision that crosses my path is made easy because of them.

Contents

Foreword

ASPERGER'S syndrome (AS) is sometimes referred to as a "hidden" disability. There is no medical or genetic test for it, adults with AS don't require curb cuts or handicapped parking spaces, you cannot spot it from twenty feet away, you can't catch it, and during casual meetings, many adults with AS may present as socially competent if a bit "quirky." Particularly within the context of a society that values social competence, however, the communicative and social deficits associated with a diagnosis of AS can, and often do, represent significant, lifelong obstacles to an individual's ability to live, work, and recreate as independently as possible. That is all very true. The book you are now holding, however, is not really an account of AS as a disability. Nor is it an account of overcoming AS as a disability. Rather it is about coming to terms with AS as a disability, pushing the limits of what that means, and educating the neurotypical world as to the intrinsic value of each one of us, independent of our varying labels.

I first met Michael John Carley on March 22, 2003, when I had the honor of moderating a panel of adults with AS at an autism conference in New York City. We had exchanged emails previously and maybe even had a phone call or two, but we had not met prior to this presentation. As it turned out, it was a meeting I would not soon forget for a variety of reasons.

March 22, you might remember, was the morning after the invasion of Iraq by coalition forces, and those of us associated with this particular conference were a little, well, jittery. In addition to our concerns for the safety of our troops and the potential implications of such an action for those of us stateside, we wondered if those who had registered for the conference would even make the trip into Manhattan for the conference given the events unfolding in the Middle East. (The majority did, by the way.) Into that context, a mere five minutes before the panel was scheduled to take the stage, walked Michael John Carley.

Someone introduced us, or maybe we introduced ourselves—I really don't remember—but Michael was clearly agitated. I thought he was upset about being late, that part of "his" AS dictated that he be on time for appointments and being late was some sort of personal failing. It certainly seemed like a reasonable assumption particularly given the fact that, at that moment, his being late was my own personal source of agitation.

As it turned out, being late really wasn't what was bothering Michael. As you will soon read in his memoir, Michael once served as a low-level diplomat charged with helping to bring potable water to some of the poorest areas of Iraq. And not only did he have friends, colleagues, and contacts in Iraq for whom he was concerned, but he had been up all night trying to get in touch with them. Further, he was politically and philosophically opposed to the invasion. Being late that day was not among his most pressing concerns.

With no time to really talk about his unease, we all assembled on stage. Michael and his three other panelists were seated at a long table, each with their own microphone, and I was standing stage right, behind the podium, ready to start our presentation. Before we began, I walked over the panelists' table to make one last check with everyone and make certain that they had everything they needed and were ready to proceed. It was at this point that Michael cupped the microphone with his hand, leaned over toward me, and said, "I have to say something. I realize it's not the best forum but I think I have to say something." Already running late and wanting to get the panel started, I simply responded, "Michael, it's your twenty minutes so say what you want."

The presentation started and each panelist was given twenty minutes to, in effect, tell their life story. Michael was the first to speak, and much to the surprise of the two hundred or so assembled parents, teachers, and related professionals in the audience, instead of offering personal insights into his life as an adult with AS, Michael launched into a ten-minute lecture about the "misguided and misconceived" (there were other, more colorful terms he used but you get the drift) U.S. policy in Iraq. He then segued into his life as an adult with AS, and the rest of the panel went off as planned.

I share with you this story as I want you understand what a truly unique person Michael John Carley is and the impact knowing him has had on my own life. Michael is an intelligent, funny, political, informed, and opinionated individual. And yes, he has Asperger's syndrome, but none of what I just said is any less true because of that. Michael is also honest to a fault. While such honesty is often characteristic of individuals with AS (to be a competent liar requires a fairly complex set of social skills), in Michael's case I always believed that his innate honesty left him little option but to offer his thoughts on world events that day.

Some people in the audience were "put off" by his lecture. For some it was the content of his lecture while for others it was the forum they saw as inappropriate. Unfortunately, both groups missed the point. Michael was simply voicing an honest opinion, and while he, along with the many others with AS, don't need curb cuts or handicapped parking slots, they do need and deserve their voices to be heard. Granted, sometimes what they have to say will not be easy to accept, but at least in my experience, it is almost always worth listening to.

There was at least one person in the audience that day who was listening very closely and that was David Tobis, the Executive Director of the Fund for Social Change, which cosponsored the conference. David was so impressed by Michael's talk (both the first and last ten minutes) that he asked to be introduced to him. From this initial meeting between Michael and David, the Global and Regional Asperger Syndrome Partnership (GRASP) was created. Michael John Carley became, and remains, the Executive Director, David Tobis assumed a seat on the Board of Directors and through the Fund for Social Change offered financial support and organization guidance, and I joined the Board as liaison to the professional community. Four years later GRASP is the largest national nonprofit run by and for adults on the spectrum. GRASP is organizationally sound and well respected in a field where our differences more often define and divide us than do our common interests serve to unite us. One could argue that GRASP has even earned the reputation as a principled voice for the autism world. This is, in no small part, due to Michael's skill as administrator, diplomat, and part-time showman. I watched as Michael took somewhat-explored ideas of self-determination, and ran with them farther than anyone thought possible. He is as results-minded an individual as you will find, once even confiding to me, "I have no desire to be a noble failure."

Michael is a unique individual in many ways. He has had a varied and successful career; he is a loving father, a doting husband, and along the way has dodged more than an occasional "social" bullet (as you will learn by reading this book). As such, he has much to offer. I know the title to this volume is *Asperger's from the Inside Out: A Supportive and Practical Guide for Anyone with Asperger's Syndrome*, but I do hope more than a few neurotypicals out there will read this volume and listen to his thoughts. I don't expect them to, nor should they, agree with everything he says just because he says it. Believe me, I certainly don't and I am pretty certain he thinks the same thing about me. But if you do take the time to listen to what he has to say, you will find some insight as well as, hopefully, some inspiration as to how to make the lives of adults with AS increasingly better. As for me, I know that I will continue to learn from, and be inspired by, Michael John Carley, and I am a far better professional and, maybe, even a far better person for knowing him.

—Peter F. Gerhardt, Ed. D.

Don't judge someone by the cards they're dealt. Judge them by how well they play the cards they're dealt.
—Michael John Carley
March 22, 2003

Introduction

MY friend was crying. He'd been fine only a minute earlier, and then suddenly he wasn't. He'd simply erupted, and I didn't know what to do.

I wondered which of my standard responses I should choose. Should I hold his hand, hug him, simply tell him it was okay, or should I instead just supportively stand close by and let him get this out of his system? Had I seen the outburst coming, I'd have been able to react. But not having witnessed a more familiar (and to me, a more organic) development of another person's emotions, I was caught off guard.

While my friend's outburst was unfamiliar, my failure to read it was not. I'd been in this predicament before—first confused by the situation, then disappointed in myself, and eventually resigned to failure. But this time was different. I wasn't thinking to myself, "Oh well . . ." and moving on blankly so as to ward off self-criticism. At this moment, unable to comfort this friend, I was suddenly sick to death of running away from *why* I was so unable. I wanted to console this friend very badly, and I couldn't.

Dr. Gobinder Singh and I were part of a three-person team in Iraq in early 2000 to choose a project site for the Iraq Water Project, a small partnership between the smaller nonprofit I worked for and the relief organization of our third delegation member. The project would repair water treatment facilities in the Basra region, Iraq's highest-need area. My organization would raise the money and get much of the publicity, and so my job was twofold for this trip: choose the site, and afterward conduct negotiations with a highly tempestuous government to allow us to be there. Dr. Singh was our "water guy," an engineer of Indian descent formerly of the United Nations Educational, Scientific, and Cultural Organization (UNESCO) who'd once been UNESCO's clean water development person in Bangladesh. His job with us was to assess the accuracy of what few feasibility studies were available (to help determine cost) and to make sure the water wouldn't be diverted for military purposes. Trips like these were tense, but the three of us were close thanks to the bonding power of shared purpose.

Three nights before this moment, we'd been in Amman, Jordan, preparing for the trip, and I'd been invited by my Muslim colleagues to accompany them at services the next morning at Amman's largest mosque. I was thrilled. I proudly accepted invitations into the churches, synagogues, and temples of friends, but I was also somewhat intimidated. The Muslim service wasn't one where you just sat, listened, or remained silent while others vocalized—you participated through gesture, which disallowed the possibility of hiding one's inequities. To prepare me, and ease my concerns of offending anyone, Dr. Singh stayed up with me most of that prior night, teaching me the hand signals that were part of the prayer service, as well as the larger meaning of each motion.

But on this particular morning, now in Iraq, we'd just finished touring Basra's main hospital, specifically the ward filled with children who would die from the waterborne diseases that political stalemating kept alive. We'd brought candy, we'd brought toys, we'd slipped money to parents, and we talked sweetly but ineffectively with the children, who in return could say little. And soon after the tour, in some room where the two of us waited for our third to return, my friend unexpectedly broke down.

Everyone's different in these situations. There are some who wear their heart on their shirtsleeve, and some who have seen so much that they have either internalized the trauma, or they have shut themselves off from it. My career in this field wasn't a long one, but I'd seen enough of both instances to realize that one's reaction to such heartbreaking sights told very little about his or her job performance. It wasn't unique that Dr. Singh had broken down uncontrollably. And it wasn't unique that I hadn't the slightest inclination to follow. What was perhaps unique on this day was my inability to communicate that it was okay for him to cry. This inability likely led my friend to believe I thought less of him; that I was wondering what was going on with him, when in fact I was finally wondering what was going on with me.

The words *Asperger's syndrome* (AS) had just been introduced to my family through my son. Consequently, those words were also moving toward me. Nobody was yet diagnosed, but our household was on to something—something very big. And acknowledging how much I'd run from my peer differences was the first step toward my properly facing the oncoming diagnosis. So aside from the natural drama already inherent in the Iraq Water

Project, there I was, additionally carrying a strong premonition of change.

My life's goal at the time was to be a successful playwright. But my "stupid day job" as a minor-league diplomat certainly beat waiting tables. I was what's called a "nongovernmental representative" of a nonprofit to the United Nations, which in essence made me one of thousands of lower-tier Ambassadors to the U.N. sent by organizations, not countries. I loved it. Everyone told you exactly how to address others, what to wear, and no one cared how you got the job done—only that it got done. There was too much at stake to care whether Carley had hurt someone's feelings, or stepped on the boss's toes . . . or so I thought at the time.

Months passed. Then, three weeks before my scheduled diagnostic appointment with Dr. Richard Perry and four months before I would take a challenging delegation of veterans on another trip back into Iraq, I said something to friends about "job burnout," and left town. I was lying somewhat; it wasn't job burnout. That tremendous wave of AS confirmation was getting closer, and it was overwhelming me. So in an uncharacteristic feat of financial recklessness, using money I didn't have (yet with my wife's blessing), I put a five-day surfing trip to Mexico on a credit card and left to go be alone with the tsunami of thoughts I was living with.

I don't surf well. I, in fact, still have yet to stand successfully on a board. But I've never cared. Water is the only arena where I have felt physically graceful, and I especially love waves. I love the deep pounding you feel, the laughter that emanates from playing in them; the sensory deep-tissue massage they inadvertently provide; the drama of "the big one" coming; and the larger, mitigating idea of giving in to that which you have no control over (nature). I enjoyed this vacation like no other. Every day I left Cabo san Lucas and drove miles up the coast to return to an isolated spot that a surfing agency had recommended, renting a board for $5 a day from a teenager who sat and happily smoked pot all day in his little shack. For five days I ate only oranges at lunchtime in the extreme heat, thinking in between the humbling lessons of the water. And as I sat and ate my fruit, I listened.

One night I "hit the town" in Cabo, in as much as a non-drinking, monogamous nondancer can do. And as I walked aimlessly, anthropologically soaking in others' revelry, I heard the faint noises of thumping music and shouting coming from a club one block away. Uncharacteristically, I walked toward it. I tried to rationalize why in heaven's name I was heading in the direction of such irritating noises, noises that grew louder and more indecipherable as I drew closer. But something was telling me to go in.

I arrived at the door to the club, and noticed in awe how it vibrated threateningly, repeatedly hammered by unimaginative bass lines. And as the doors opened, I was jolted by the sudden acceleration of volume, and by the sight of hundreds of people, mostly young, swaying, gyrating, sweating, and drinking recklessly on multiple floor levels. Against my instincts I walked in, determined to absorb it all.

My movements were slow, more careful and methodical than others', relaxed in contrast to the bodies whipping back and forth. Yet, oddly, few people bumped into me, and I began to feel like a ghost that no one saw. I walked the room, climbed up to the many floors, and viewed the ground-floor scene of tourist masses from many vantage points. All the while I was slowly taking mental notes; notes that weren't as smugly jotted down as they'd been in the past. For as I watched the dictionaries of non-verbal communication flowing back and forth, I was hit fully, finally, that what separated me from them wasn't cultural. It never had been. It wasn't intellectual. It never had been. It was bigger than that.

At that moment, one month before the confirmation of a formal diagnosis, I knew. Staring into that sea of abandon (a picture seared into my memory), I knew. I realized I had Asperger's syndrome.

───────────

IT is now almost seven years after that alienating night. Now I run GRASP, the Global and Regional Asperger Syndrome Partnership, the world's largest organization of adults diagnosed along the autism spectrum. Shortly after my diagnosis, and two years before GRASP was formed, I took over a New York City support group network and watched it grow from twelve people in circulation, to over four hundred in just two years' time. During these years, stories of other adult diagnoses poured in, and I quickly saw that I was not alone. Then in 2003, the Fund for Social Change provided us with the start-up funding to begin GRASP, and as the number of our regional groups grew and I traveled to run them, more stories surfaced. And when GRASP expanded its networks farther across the country, with other people besides myself running them, it became clear that there were stories everywhere.

All in all, I arguably may have listened to more stories about being diagnosed as an adult than anyone. Such potential boasting aside, I relate this simply as someone who is in awe of the stories themselves. This process, this coming to terms with the diagnosis, is beyond most people's imaginations. It is a journey not given anywhere near the weight or attention it deserves. If not run from, this process causes an individual to look back and review nearly everything that's gone on before; it causes positive but difficult changes; it evokes positive but difficult reinterpretations of memories; and it removes much blame. Most importantly, it provides the first realistic chance at change for the better.

It changes everything, and not just for the diagnosees. It also changes things for the people in their lives.

There are essays available on various aspects of the process, good ones too, but not one solid book exists that clearly and chronologically outlines the whole tumultuous path. And if soon to be or recently diagnosed individuals have at least some idea of what lies before them—a printed guide to prepare them, showing the many others who have gone through this too—then the process will be eased.

That's the professional obligation I feel. Yet I'm also the father of a child with AS—a father who demands a better, more behaviorally permissive world available for his son when he grows up.

But lastly, and more selfishly, I have yet to see a diagnosed individual that was as flat-out dumb lucky as I was. Compared with others whom I've watched weather this process, I am one of the least amazing stories of relative accomplishment you'll find; for there is no quantum leap from my original place on the autism spectrum compared to where I am now. I was mind-bogglingly fortunate in the jobs I chose, professions that unknowingly improved certain AS challenges. I was lucky in the people I drifted toward, lucky in the thicker skin I'd built up with which to navigate what, I can only now admit, was a very confusing world. There may be something to be learned from how a theatre career taught me to better see from another's perspective, or iron out motor skills issues. There may be something to be learned from being raised in a card-playing family, where restraint and picking up on body signals would prevent you from losing your allowance. There may be something to be learned from travel, and work, in both destitute and nondestitute cultures that instills in you the comforting realization that one size does not fit all. Whether this is "sole survivor guilt," or instead something more positive, these conscience-driven impulses only add to an already overinflated sense of purpose.

My personal contributions to this book are therefore numerous, perhaps too much so. That said, however, they appear amid contributions by GRASP members and alongside excerpts written by already established authors, material that is all there to solely serve or illustrate the content. For this is not a memoir. This is a book born from GRASP—what it has seen, the similarities and the differences, the patterns, and the exceptions.

This book is written primarily for that adult; to ease them on that long road. But it also exists to enlighten their loved ones, or their clinicians, with an account that suggests much of what the diagnosed person might be going through. Even if my writing proves inadequate, the subject material alone is of enormous importance. The remarkable positive changes that have embraced my life, and the lives of countless others, are not to be missed. The buckets of explanations, redemption, relief, and blamelessness far outweigh the negatives that these revelations provide.

I would expect that most of the people who read this book will do so on behalf of themselves, or on behalf of an individual they care about. But for one brief moment, don't think only of yourself, or whomever you have in mind as you read. Think big—just once, right now—and look at the numbers of potentially affected people, and all their underutilized talents . . . Greater society is an equal beneficiary when those recently diagnosed individuals courageously put their shoes on, and walk down this path.

—Michael John Carley
New York City
July 2007

CHAPTER ONE

What Is Asperger's Syndrome?

Only that day dawns to which we are awake.
—Henry David Thoreau

***

The Big Picture

ASPERGER'S syndrome is a neurological condition. It is one of five diagnoses that comprise what's called "the autism spectrum," which also includes autism and pervasive developmental disorder–not otherwise specified (PDD-NOS). Named after the Austrian clinician Dr. Hans Asperger, who first identified it in 1944, Asperger's syndrome (AS) may have influenced Albert Einstein, Thomas Edison, Wolfgang Amadeus Mozart, and Glenn Gould—among many others. But the more isolating characteristics can seriously reduce an individual's prospects for a happy, fulfilling life.

AS is characterized primarily by:

1. Deficits in social interaction and nonverbal communication, or the inability to instinctively understand social cues the

way the rest of the world does—cues, signals, or methods of sharing that play such a huge role in our everyday world.

2. Difficulties to varying degrees with the concept that some-one else isn't thinking the same thing as you are (also called "mind-blindness" or "The Theory of Mind").

Having AS, autism, or PDD can mean having great abilities, but it can also mean never leaving the home of one's parents, never holding down a job for any extended period of time, and perhaps never enjoying a satisfying intimate relationship. Yet if these conditions were understood on a broad level, circum-stances would enable most diagnosees to lead happy and pro-ductive lives.

Characteristics

There is a long list of characteristics that may point to an indi-vidual having AS. Not one of these clues is an automatic "you've got it," and not one of these ingredients, if missing, means "you don't." Passionate interests, at least one sensory integration chal-lenge, and difficulty engaging in reciprocal conversation can be key markers, but the real list is extensive.

The following table outlines the behavioral indicators that might or might not match the diagnosee. It is drawn in such a way to show these elements as vulnerable to both positive and contradictorily negative interpretations.

Characteristic	Negative Interpretation	Positive Interpretation
Intense absorption in a topic or field of interest.	Individual is obsessed, and is driven further into this absorption by anxiety and stress.	Individual is passionate about a topic or field of interest.
Inability to read nonverbal communications such as facial expressions, body gestures, and shifting vocal tones.	Many miscommunications with the neurotypical world are guaranteed, leading to failed socialization and lost opportunities.	In most cases, the ability at communicating using text—either in reading or writing—is heightened, albeit in an often too-literal sense.
Professorial, monotoned manner of speaking.	Stilted awkwardness that is off-putting to others, often preventing further steps in a potential relationship.	Focused on being clear in what is being said by utilizing a strength, text.
Discomfort or inability at small talk. Sees no logic in it.	Off-putting and impolite.	Gets to the point. For many, this is very refreshing.
Difficulty in recognizing faces (also known as "face-blindedness").	Individual is rude or uncaring for not making the effort to remember someone. An annoyance or inconvenience for everyone involved, including the individual.	Nothing more than an annoyance or inconvenience, involving no intended slight to anyone.
Motor skills issues such as illegible handwriting and poor coordination, balance, and bodily rhythm.	Physical awkwardness resulting in teasing, difficulty at sports, and further isolation, which discourages the individual from not just socialization, but also (to name just one possibility) exercise, sometimes for life. Handwriting issue often has the individual appearing uncaring, if not disturbed.	We are doing less and less handwriting as computer use continues to grow and dominate our daily lives. And if these differences were conveyed to the world as the nonthreatening issues they really are, socialization would be made far easier. However, very little good can be said of no exercise.

Characteristic	Negative Interpretation	Positive Interpretation
Inflexibility. Need for routine. Dislikes change.	An inconvenience for those in contact with the individual. Can also lead to anxiety and/or trauma in the individual when change is mandatory.	Focused more on the routine task than the next person. Also, the sense of order caused by routine can be very calming, and can reduce the anxiety caused by living in a world that confuses you.
Greater than normal abilities at math, science, art, or music.	Exclusion of other subjects.	The individual is talented at math, science, art, or music.
Problems with imagination—may have played out most noticeably when the individual was a child, as a difficulty with "imaginative play" (my son would often spin the wheels of his toy car to see how they worked rather than imagine himself driving it).	Varying degrees of inability toward imagination and creative or flexible thinking.	May be indications of a great technical mind.
Problems with nonartistic activities or fields of study.	Can be seen as "goofing off" or not focused enough on serious matters.	May be indications of a great creative mind.
Poor ability at eye contact.	Can be interpreted as disingenuous, shifty, or uncaring if the neurotypical recipient believes that eye contact is a courtesy he is entitled to.	Individual may hear better because of movement of head. Very often this is due to a sensory integration involving unique hearing, and not eyesight. However, it can also be that, for some, concentrating on both another person's face and simultaneously trying to listen can be exhausting.

Characteristic	Negative Interpretation	Positive Interpretation
Says whatever comes into their head, unaware of the potential damage the statement might cause.	The individual is rude.	The individual is honest.
Penchant for interrupting others.	The individual is rude.	The individual has something to say, another indicator that social contact is indeed desired.
Sensory issues: difficulty processing certain types of lighting, certain smells, tastes, fabrics, or noises.	Individual appears broken, or can scare other people who don't understand the motivations behind the reactions or increased inflexibility.	Frequently correctable with environmental changes.
Stimming: involuntary reflex actions such as flapping the hands or feet, rocking, or making noises.	Individual appears broken, or can scare other people who don't understand the motivations behind the reactions.	Cognitive awareness and loss in anxiety can help redirect some stims to become more socially accepted, although "stims" generally tend to stick around to some degree for life. But stims are harmful to no one, and are often an expression of pleasure.
Difficulty in staying on a topic and following the thread of the ongoing conversation.	Individual is thought of as impatient or selfish. Can be due to a difficulty with short-term memory (see below).	Individual may simply not be interested in the topic.
Repeating of favorite topics or songs; watching favored movies repeatedly.	Annoying to others. Limits the scope of learning to fewer songs, topics, etc., than most people.	An attempt to soak up as much as possible about things that the individual admires and wants to embody.

Characteristic	Negative Interpretation	Positive Interpretation
Difficulty understanding figures of speech, euphemisms, and analogies.	Individual appears unintelligent, and can be further ostracized from social contact due to his inability to "join in."	Again, consequence of literal-mindedness, or "text-only" disposition. Can be dealt with by cognitively understanding how these colloquial uses of words or idioms work. What can also help is the individual gaining insight into why people employ them.
Bad at processing recently learned information.	Individual appears incapable of improvement, or has naturally bad short-term memory.	This is often a trade, as the long-term memory is notoriously quite good. However, reductions in anxiety or switching to topics of interest may do much to assist the individual with short-term memory.
"Shutdowns," or in more dramatic situations, meltdowns.	Can drive frustrated others away, and/or lead to lost opportunities.	Reductions in anxiety and stress will help. And the individual knowing why he himself is undergoing such anxiety—knowing more and more about the diagnosis—will reduce the stress, as well as finding out why the individual is frustrated.
Difficulty understanding "consequences" of behavioral differences.	Further lost opportunities.	If explained in a noncritical manner, the idea of consequences, ramifications, cause and effect, and why the cause and effect are so different for others . . . all this will do much toward improvement.

Characteristic	Negative Interpretation	Positive Interpretation
Long monologues when the other person in the conversation wants them to stop.	The individual is rude.	The individual is interested, and passionate, about the topic.
Is fooled easily.	Easily duped by tricks, pranks, or scams, possibly causing great social and/or financial harm. This confusion adds to possible anger and stress overload.	The individual is trusting and loyal.
Difficulty processing accumulated stress, anxiety, or anger.	Accumulated frustrations will often sit, and gather, until they are either triggered, or until the overload of these bad experiences boils over. When the inevitable outburst happens, others mistakenly look for what had happened *at that moment*. And they can't find anything specific because the tension has built up over time. Individual is then thought of as dramatically more disturbed than he or she really is.	Individual is often bravely trying to get by in situations that are obviously not right for him, or that have not been explained properly. Learning to identify and process one's own emotions will help.

It should be noted that the existence of a "Positive Interpretation" column does not reduce the need for change and/or assimilation if the individual wants to succeed more in the neurotypical world. And it should also be noted that the "Positive" column does not often come to fruition when an individual has been made to feel bad about what separates him or her from the rest of the world.

Also, while stress, anxiety, and anger were mentioned at the end of this list, their many possible consequences were not. Getting flustered easily, having difficulty driving a car, anger toward certain relatives—these are often realities in the day-to-day living of someone with AS, but they are not direct symptoms of the condition. Experiencing life with AS in a world that does not understand it, and being constantly misunderstood as well as misunderstanding others—this is what causes these characteristics, not the diagnosis itself. Accumulated traumas and stress will always cause a person to retreat and become less and less trusting of future instruction or assistance. For when adults get diagnosed—as opposed to when children get diagnosed—it comes after they have been around the block awhile, and "the block" probably had some banana peels strewn underfoot.

At GRASP, we try to pose the following question to our members, asking them how it relates to them: *Look at the individual who sits at the computer all day. Is he that way because that's who he is? Or because every time he tried to make a friend, it ended badly, and one day, somewhere inside, he just said "I quit"?* The answers, as you can imagine, vary wildly.

In addition to stress, anxiety, and anger, several myths were intentionally left off the list.

WHAT IS ASPERGER'S SYNDROME? 19

Myths About the Autism Spectrum

Individuals on the autism spectrum have no emotion

It's there. Emotion is sometimes prohibited from surfacing by our failing to identify either those emotions or emotionally charged circumstances as they happen. But this myth developed because we often *display* emotion differently. Furthermore, different things can *trigger* those differently displayed emotions, often through misperceptions. Historically, because individuals on the spectrum didn't show or have emotion triggered in the same manner as everyone else, clinicians wrongly assumed that this meant the emotion didn't exist.

Individuals on the spectrum have no sense of humor

Ha-ha. Again, we may very well simply find different things to be funny, such as wordplays and mathematical inconsistencies. However, that's not to say our funny bone is completely foreign or alien. One populist form of humor that *is* enjoyed by many people on the spectrum is satire. Satire tends to make fun of greater society—welcome medicine to many for whom greater society has sometimes been unintentionally cruel. Television shows such as *The Simpsons* and *South Park* (and for us older folks, *Monty Python's Flying Circus*) can be a very realistic chance at joining the rest of the world in a shared laugh.

To give a personal example of unique humor "triggers": I personally laugh whenever I hear the French language used in rap, or rock and roll music. The timber, the inflection, or the sound of it simply strikes me as hysterically funny (this partially caused my Parisian girlfriend in college to break up with me). I love French opera, jazz, the music of Edith Piaf—I studied the language in school for six years even—but in these two forms of music, something is set off. Another uncommon "humor trigger" that has plagued me all my life is the sound of sheep bleating, or "baa-ing," as a group. There is little known predictability in what will amuse individuals on the spectrum, but something usually will.

Individuals on the autism spectrum have no sexual appetite

This actually varies. There are many for whom sexual intimacy, owing to sensory issues or just plain fear (if not accumulated trauma), can be akin to fingernails on a blackboard. But there appear to be just as many people categorized in the "insatiable-appetite" opposite.

Individuals on the spectrum have no capacity for improvement

This is a myth created by public awareness campaigns that focus only on the catastrophic damage that has occurred to certain families where there is at least one severely challenged autistic family member. The damage to these families is real, but the idea that these situations are representative of the entire world of autism is not. These horror stories constitute a small percentage, though a percentage deserving of services. Given the right supports and positive environment, we all accumulate skills that will help us either better mirror society, or adjust to our very inability to do so.

Individuals have no capacity for empathy

Actually, this is true more often than it is not. But the myth lies in the misperception of the word *empathy*. Too often it is thought to be the same as *sympathy*. Sympathy is the capacity to be concerned about how others feel. We have that, and plenty of it—but again, it just may be hard to read, or see, and will also be affected by our ability to pick up on another's emotions as they are happening. Empathy, however, is the capacity to pick up on what someone else is thinking. There, we are indeed challenged.

All individuals on the spectrum are good at math

This goes along with us all being good at science, or music. Plenty of people diagnosed are terrible at math, good at recognizing faces, and so forth. Again, no presently identified indicator—or "bullet point"—is an automatic for an individual on the spectrum to be diagnosed.

Too Broad a Spectrum?

The autism spectrum is exactly that, a spectrum. But it's a large one. The autism spectrum is complicated, and intimidating, and frustrating. It is so diverse, in fact, that pretty much everyone involved in the autism world seems to want to chop it up so as to better compartmentalize and address the differing needs of people on opposite ends of this vast gradient. Unfortunately, we can't. We can't dumb it down so as to make it easier to describe, or swallow. Autism is that complicated; and we who work in the field have to better own up to that fact if we are to become successful advocates and not confuse the world with contradictory messages, such as "this side of the spectrum needs services" versus "this side of the spectrum needs to get rid of them."

Where an individual falls on the spectrum is, oddly enough, not important. What's important is concentrating on what that individual's needs are.

In this book, I'll occasionally use words like *autism* and *the autism spectrum*, for in the end they may all mean the same thing. But primarily, as evidenced by this book's title, I will use the term *Asperger's syndrome* (AS). It is what I believe the majority of readers will have.

While everyone will have their own preference as to what word they use to define themselves, I use *Asperger's syndrome* to describe myself simply because that's what I was diagnosed with. I'm no doctor so I tend not to doubt their call. Some other folks, however—many GRASP members—call themselves *autistic* despite AS being the term used on their diagnosis, and given the logic of the spectrum, they cannot be faulted. All clinical attempts at drawing a line in the sand, where Asperger's syndrome becomes autism and vice versa, have failed in practice. Furthermore, people can develop skills that allow them to better get by in the world. So does that mean that, for someone in the middle of the spectrum, the real diagnosis could change from autism to AS because of certain improvements? That shouldn't be.

You could easily argue that no one should become married to whatever terminology exists today. Given the vast amount we still have to learn about autism, the terminology may change, and change again, and again . . . But for a diagnosis to change based on one's capacity (or desire) to better mirror the rest of the world leaves the label feeling like it's part of a grading system rather than being a legitimate diagnosis. This condition is primarily genetic. The wiring an individual has is what she'll die with, though she can dramatically improve her lot in life.

When we say "genetic," there are two important factors to consider:

1. Just because the gene(s) passes through generations in families doesn't mean that everyone touched will qualify for a full diagnosis. It appears a very random roll of the dice whether someone will have a full-blown case of autism, show traits, or show nothing (effectively then being only a carrier pigeon for the gene).

2. Though genetic, autism spectrum conditions have demonstrated that there can be environmental triggers that "set the autism off." Proof of this are sensory integration issues, which by themselves are indeed environmental triggers.

GRASP, for instance, spells out "Asperger Syndrome" in its title, but it does so more for reasons of strategy than authenticity. Asperger's is what the vast majority of our members are diagnosed with. But our aim is to embrace those main three diagnoses of the autism spectrum: Asperger's syndrome, autism, and the lesser-used PDD-NOS.

So let me now try to make these complexities a little easier to swallow . . .

Here's our "spectrum":

It looks a little boring right now.

So let's think of Albert Einstein as the pinnacle of autistic achievement and put him on the farthest end of the spectrum.

Albert Einstein

And now on the vast other end, let's think of someone non-verbal, who has been unable to respond to any of the available therapies or treatments, and who needs assistance to do pretty much everything that neurotypicals do in their average day—someone who could be flat-out brilliant, but whom we've not yet learned how to communicate with.

A nonverbal individual   Albert Einstein
who does not respond to
any known treatments,
someone whom we're
yet to learn how to
communicate with

This autism spectrum, remember, has little to do with natural intelligence. It has to do mostly with wiring, but also an ability (or level of desire) to mirror how the rest of the world does things, often thought of as "functionality level" (in GRASP support groups, I'll often refer to this lightly as "how much of 'the juice' you've got"). But too often, more challenged individuals are thought of as useless when it is we who so far have been unable to tap into what's there.

Many of those near the Einstein end of things would often prefer a separation of diagnoses because they do not want to regard the more-affected individual as anything like them-selves. Their capacity for positive self-imagery is enough at risk as it is.

The great comic/tragic thing is that many people on the oppo-site end often couldn't agree more. More-challenged individuals are often terrified and intimidated by the notion that they will be expected to duplicate the achievements of, say, a lawyer with AS who has four kids and a mortgage.

GRASP tries to blend in people from all walks of the spec-trum because we believe we can all learn much from one an-other. And although our structured support meetings do not address the comfort levels of many challenged individuals on the spectrum,* we accommodate the vast majority, and succeed with them more often than not. But our mission of shared ex-perience and mutual learning often works against the afore-mentioned fear of "the other side," a very human need that revolves around an individual's sense of identity, which can seem especially fragile at the time of diagnosis. Words like *As-perger's* or *autism* carry stigmas—large ones. And these stigmas don't just come from the outside. They are also felt internally, by us. These are prejudices we *all* grew up with, and we will succeed far more once these stigmas have been done away with. They are not just mean, or damaging. They are also unneces-sary, even if they grew to fruition under humane and inevitable circumstances.

It is for this reason that in 2005 GRASP stopped using the term *high-functioning* in its literature, and why you will not see it in the remainder of this book (unless in quotes from other

---

* Modeling and visual aids—such as videos that demonstrate rather than orally com-municate lessons—are often the prerequisites to becoming able to benefit from (and enjoy) such meetings.

sources). While prefacing any diagnosis with *high-functioning* may clandestinely communicate that "all is not lost," we have to find other ways to provide that same hopefulness. When someone is high-functioning, someone else then has to be low-functioning, and we know enough about autism now to know that we are discussing people who can read what's written about them, and who can hear what's said about them. All negative terminology hurts, and hearing negative references to oneself would impede the progress of anyone, no matter where their abilities place them on the spectrum. Furthermore, if a natural intelligence of a unique nature is indeed there inside those more-challenged individuals, then to call them low-functioning wouldn't just damage self-esteem, it also then becomes inaccurate.

For the record, after I was diagnosed, I went through the same fear. At the first support group meeting I attended, I realized I was in the company of two folks significantly more affected than I. And I was immediately petrified: "Whoa! That's *not* me!" But I very quickly saw in them something amazing: exaggerated versions of gestures that I had done my whole life, gestures that had been called "nervous" by the adults in my childhood. And as a consequence in that childhood, I'd grown up believing that I was a nervous person, even though many of my actions suggested otherwise. Thanks to that support meeting, I saw that these gestures had always been my AS at work, confirming what I'd long suspected was not nervousness.

No matter where an individual falls on this spectrum, it makes sense to hold tightly to the idea that at no time will the individual's ability to improve cease. A person's success as an autistic spectrum individual trying to succeed must be measured by relative proportion to where he or she originally falls on the spectrum.

The Human Factor of the *DSM-IV*

The *DSM-IV* (the fourth edition of the *Diagnostic and Statistical Manual of Mental Disorders*) is the psychiatric professional's source for definitions of diagnosis. It is what the diagnostician consults to figure out what sets you apart from others. The book isn't perfect. But if clinicians didn't use this volume, and instead relied on their instincts, we'd have mayhem, and far greater inconsistencies in diagnosis than exist already today.

Reading this book's definition of AS can leave the impression that the authors think we are all robotic hedonists. But the clinical value of the diagnosis, and the very inclusion of AS into this fourth edition (published in 1994), is rapidly changing the world for the better.

Most of the clinicians that GRASP works with agree that two flaws exist in the *DSM-IV*, flaws that we hope will be taken care of for the publication of the *DSM-V*, whenever that will be.

In addition to AS, autism, and PDD-NOS, the *DSM-IV* lists two other conditions—Rett's disorder and childhood disintegrative disorder (CDD)—giving the autism spectrum a total of five diagnoses. The *DSM-IV*, like all books, was put together by humans, with human faults. And the first flaw is believed to be that it was a mistake to include Rett's and CDD on the autism spectrum. Conditions such as nonverbal learning disorder (NLD), attention-deficit hyperactivity disorder (ADHD), and possibly even fragile X syndrome would seem to have far more justification for inclusion in the autism spectrum than these other two.

Second, the defining criteria list bullet-pointed characteristics of AS, as do most books about Asperger's. And they ask the diagnostician to find those elements that the individual has, the ones they don't have, and then, based on that information, to make the diagnosis. This is fine when diagnosing children. But many adults, as they go to be evaluated, do not have a third component taken into consideration—through either painful peer pressure or sheer hard work, they were able to compensate for the bullet points that they *once* had and because of that, they learned to better mirror greater society. The consequences of our lives lived, and the products of adult experience, are therefore not taken into consideration. These characteristics will be missed by the diagnostician unless they are verbally communicated (and believed) during the diagnostic session, and that's only if the adult being considered is even aware of them. Many clinicians compensate by including family members, preferably parents (by phone even), in the diagnostic process of an adult, and most of the time this adjustment allows for an accurate diagnosis. But hopefully, future editions of the *DSM* will take adult concerns into far better consideration.

Summary

Simply the best description of AS I've ever heard came from a five-year-old boy . . .

Young Dylan Braxton Hamilton was getting examined by his pediatrician. The two had a very good rapport with one another. He could tease Dylan a little, and it was okay. So he half-jokingly told Dylan, "I know what's going on with you; you've just got too many wires."

Dylan said, "No doctor, my problem is that the wires aren't insulated well enough."

IF the Centers for Disease Control and Prevention's (CDC) figure of 1 out of every 150 people diagnosed with some form of autism is accurate, and if the United States is populated by 300 million people, then 2 million Americans have a diagnosis on the autism spectrum. You are not alone.

Arguments are continuing as to whether the conditions are completely genetic, or whether they are genetic predispositions that can be triggered by environmental circumstances. There are even some who believe we got it from completely different sources other than genetics, though most of the sane world disregards these ideas. Even if Mom or Dad were simply carriers of the gene (and may or may not qualify for a diagnosis, or even have traits), it appears we still got it from Mom or Dad.

Research continues on the frontal and temporal lobes of the brain, right hemisphere cortical dysfunction, serotonin levels of the brain, and so on, in an effort to be able to physically spot that gene, or combination of genes. But there is so much to learn in genetic and neurological research. And prior to satisfying our desire to scientifically and intellectually understand the autism spectrum fully, we have to address the needs of the many people, alive now, who are in great distress. This multitude of potentially contributing human beings deserve the higher priority. Furthermore, greater society could use them.

Asperger's syndrome is not a mental illness, and it's not a disease. It is a neurological condition that sets us apart from most of the people on the planet in both good and bad ways. Dr. Tony Attwood, my personal favorite among the clinical book authors, doesn't even use the term *diagnosis* when he evaluates his clients. He prefers the term *discovery*. And assuming you have just been or are recently diagnosed, you are embarking on what is probably the greatest discovery of your life thus far.

Welcome.

CHAPTER TWO

Now I Know: What the Diagnosis Feels Like

But sometimes I get fed up with my spiritual existence. Instead of
forever hovering above, I'd like to feel there's some weight to me,
and to end my eternity and bind me to earth. Each step, each gust
of wind, I'd like to be able to say, "Now!" "Now!" and "Now!"
—Wim Wenders, *Wings of Desire*

To say that this discovery was a bombshell wouldn't be an exaggeration: it was a life-changing event. It reinterpreted most of my life in a new, understandable, and logical way. As with everything else in life, I would rather know the truth about things, the reason why something is happening in a certain way: and now, for the first time, I could understand why things had happened in certain way. Even though I still have some of the difficulties associated with Asperger Syndrome, it helps 100 percent to know why I am different.
—Jen Birch, *Congratulations! It's Asperger Syndrome*

On one trip to the bookstore I came across a book about Asperger's Syndrome . . . After about 15 minutes of reading about AS, my jaw dropped to the floor. I said very audibly in the store,

"Hallelujah!" . . . I felt an immense wave of relief wash over me as everything suddenly made sense. I looked back over my life, [through] all the painful memories that could now be explained . . . Getting a diagnosis can be very a cathartic experience . . . Those hidden barriers between you and others that seemed like a mystery over the years will finally be understood . . . It made me feel both better and worse knowing that I hadn't meant to disturb or hurt anyone.

—Nick Dubin, *Breaking Through Hidden Barriers*

As I read through the article my first reaction was relief. It was as if I had a weight lifted off my shoulders. I had every single "symptom" on this checklist. I read it and reread it, then said to Mum, "Do you think I could have AS?" She simply said, "Yes you have." I must admit I did think "Well, thanks a lot for telling me" but the relief was most definitely stronger than the annoyance.

—Thirteen-year-old Luke Jackson,
Freaks, Geeks & Asperger Syndrome

Slowly I read the pamphlet and then scanned the "instant diagnosis" checklist that I had come to regard as psychiatric fast food . . . After all this time—this was who I was! There is a reason for this! There are other people like this! This is nothing I did, this is not my fault, I am not lazy, or crazy, or wrong—this is the way I came!

—Todd J. Schmidt, "Jordan's Gift,"
from *Voices on the Spectrum*

Finally getting the right label was one of the best things that has ever happened to me . . . It is a story of how I emerged from the darkness of [autism] into the beauty of [autism].

—Dawn Prince Hughes, *Songs of the Gorilla Nation*

I have finally reached the end of my race to be normal. And that was exactly what I needed. A finish—an end to the pretending that had kept me running in circles for most of my life.

—Liane Holliday Willey, *Pretending to Be Normal*

As these quotes reflect, being diagnosed with AS is often accompanied by an overwhelming sense of relief. For now there's explanation for all those incidents you walked away from scratching your head. Now there's the realization that maybe you weren't as much to blame for "Incident A" as you, and others, might have previously thought. Now there can be so much release . . . These are wonderful, liberating feelings, the likes of which I don't have the fullest words to describe. There will be "cons" to accompany these "pros"—there are with everyone. But in being granted this new lens to view yourself, the overriding effect is more positive than negative.

Yet this isn't the experience of everyone, and the reasons behind predominantly negative reactions vary. For instance, older individuals, in their fifties and beyond, often feel the diagnosis will have less impact on their future. It may illuminate much of the past, but some wonder how much change they can reasonably expect to gain from the diagnosis once they are in their more advanced years. Teenagers and young adults might also feel too overwhelmed with identity issues as they go through the developmental journey of finding out who they are. Furthermore, there are long-suffering individuals who have endured years of inaccurate, more heavily stigmatized diagnoses such as schizophrenia, to name just one. Instead of relief, they might be overwhelmed with anger if they suffered through histories of unnecessary pharmaceuticals, the consequential side effects of those pharmaceuticals, or inaccurately mandated institutionalizations.

But the largest barrier any individual faces lies in feeling broken and second-rate because of the stigma associated with the word *autism*.

Origin of a Stigma: A Very Brief History of Autism

Autism spectrum conditions are disorders. And *disorder*, to be honest, is a word I personally try to refrain from using, feeling that any word with a prefix of *dis* is bound to have a psychologically negative effect. But we have to call it for what it is. The autism spectrum presents one as destined to be in the behavioral minority. And as much as we're going to rationally examine the logic and the sociological rationale behind the development of such stigma, having had this condition all along has made life primarily harder, not easier. The world works in a certain way, and not fitting into the mold of the majority presents challenges. The diagnosis is both an answer, and a call. A call to make changes (so long as the individual chooses to) now that we finally have accurate information, and the right tools. Beforehand it was like trying to fix a car with a toolbox meant for a bicycle.

Autism was first defined by American child psychiatrist Leo Kanner back in 1943. And to a less-publicized degree, Austrian clinician Hans Asperger identified Asperger's syndrome only one year later in 1944.

Dr. Kanner's definitions revolved around an inability to use verbal communication, a preference for objects over people, and a dislike of breaks in routines. However, he also believed that there was a higher than normal intelligence level lurking inside the autistic brain. Dr. Asperger's findings included an inability to

So did autism and AS exist before the 1940s, when they were identified? Of course. In the millenniums before Kanner and Asperger, we
can guess that people were erroneously thought of as psychotic,
mentally retarded, lazy, comic, shy, eccentric, and so on. The scope of
such history-wide misunderstanding is a very hard concept to even
imagine.

---

pick up nonverbal communication, passionate interests, motor
skills difficulties, and an oddly exhibited use of the spoken
word. While Kanner's work gained in notoriety, Asperger's did
not. Probably because of the lingering stigma of conducting his
work in Nazi Austria, Asperger's work wasn't translated into
English until the early 1980s.

But in the 1950s, Kanner's theories of intelligence inside the
autistic brain began to come under fire, and were eventually dis-
counted. Clinicians couldn't see the intelligence, and couldn't tap
into it, so the idea that the intelligence couldn't exist grew and
grew. Only today, as we learn more and more ways to communicate with the autistic brain (through behavioral therapies, social
skills curriculums, and so on), have his ideas regained respect.
Like their inability to see humor and emotion, doctors believed
in the intelligence only when they could spot it.

But Kanner was no geneticist. He believed that bad parenting
was a very possible cause of autism, and he recommended placements outside the home for autistic children, an idea that a man
named Bruno Bettelheim would take tragically further.

Bruno Bettelheim, a survivor of the Dachau concentration
camp, came into prominence as a child psychologist in the
1960s. He is most famous for coining the term *refrigerator
mothers* to describe what he felt were mothers whose perceived

lack of affection was causing their child's autism. Acting on his theories, Bettelheim was responsible for separating families for periods of up to two years, often subjecting the autistic individuals to deplorable conditions. But as ludicrous as we now know this notion of loveless mothers to be, Dr. Thomas L. Whitman in his book *The Development of Autism: A Self-Regulatory Perspective* provides a possible explanation for the origins of such poorly thought out ideas:

> Perhaps influenced by his own personal history as a prisoner in a Nazi concentration camp, Bettelheim saw children with autism as victims of environmental trauma.

Having seen the change in behavior of his fellow prisoners as they endured unspeakable hardships, Bettelheim had perhaps become fixated on change brought about by one's surroundings and/or suffering. Such thinking would explain his inability to consider hereditary means or predetermined events.

The harm he caused was very real. Whether it was damage to the families that came across him, or a greater damage to the iconography associated with words like *autism*, his beliefs dominated the thinking of the 1960s and early 1970s. And the negative stature of autism made it seem logical to do everything in your power to avoid your child being labeled autistic.

While Oliver Sacks does not condone Bettelheim's summarizations, he has defended Bettelheim's talent for observing behaviors.* And in a comic moment of "oops," GRASP was once turned down for a particular grant because we briefly criticize "Bettelheimian thinking" in almost all of our grant proposals—

---

* Heard in person at the November 2003 conference at the Seaver Autism Center at Mt. Sinai Hospital in New York.

and the Board of Directors of this one foundation turned out to be old friends of his. So the infamous doctor still has his circles of support. But overall, the world realized very quickly what nonsense the refrigerator mother theory was, and almost overnight, a new movement—if we can call it that, for it was more unconscious than organized—arose to counter the devastation his ideas had brought. We'll call this new ideology the "Why do you want to put a label on him?" movement, or "Antilabelism."

Given that words like *autism* carried such negative potential, the motives behind antilabelism were justified. If the word carries such meaning, then don't use the word. So the new trend became calling people of varying conditions *special*, if they were to be called anything. Loving children for who they were, whatever that may be, and negating any attempts to attach diagnoses became the new strategy for handling individuals on the autism spectrum. By keeping the aura surrounding the individual vague and undefined, no one could ascribe anything harmful to the family dynamic.

This well-intended movement successfully implemented a quick rebuttal to Bettelheim's thinking. However, in a comic/tragic twist of irony, these "new" ideas only furthered the damage to words like *autism*. For in avoiding these "labels," the perpetuators of these ideas still implied that there was something decidedly wrong with someone if a diagnosis along the autism spectrum was accurate. The shame, even on a subconscious level, was still there. Discussing the diagnosis only in fearful whispers added to Bettelheim's impact that the word *autism* implied only negative outcomes.

Antilabelism argued that the potential for individualism was lost when someone became stamped with a diagnosis; and that this so-called label would categorize him or her in such a way as to deny that person's humanity. This interpretation implies that diagnosis itself is a be-all and end-all of who the person is, and this is wrong. Diagnosis is not intended as a eulogy, but almost instead as a starting point, a context, or a filter *through* which to discover the person's individuality—far quicker than without it. A diagnosis, for instance, shouldn't mean "you can't do [a certain activity]." It rather means that the individual will be less able to do the activity, but that he probably could, especially if he works much harder at it than the next person. Going in the opposite extreme, and demonizing diagnosis itself, was unfortunately our society's flawed answer to Bettelheim's legacy. It not only perpetuated the stigma, it also prevented anyone from achieving self-advocacy skills—because no one knew what they had. Even the word *special*, over the years, has now been changed in our collective lexicon into something far more condescending than it is supportive.

The iconography around these words can be improved upon, but so too can the iconography of the *behaviors* of autism. For whether or not there's a word attached to irregular behaviors and movements, those behaviors and movements will stigmatize the individual just as much as the diagnosis will. People don't need to see a diagnostic evaluation to know that something is unfamiliar in someone crossing the street who has motor coordination issues caused by a neurological condition.

In 2004, GRASP began a relationship with the New York City Public Schools' Special Education District, known as District 75. And despite the fact that these were more challenged kids than what we'd experienced in GRASP support groups, I still expected something similar to the peer-run groups we hold for adults. But when I entered the room of students for the first time, I quickly sensed something was wrong.

"Do you guys know why you're here?" I finally asked.

Silence. Maybe a few kids shook their heads.

"Great," I'm thinking. "No one told them why they were coming."

"Well," I began, "we're here because all of us, including me, are diagnosed somewhere on the autism spectrum. We all either have autism, Asperger's syndrome, or PDD. Which one do each of you have?"

Silence.

They didn't know. Ranging in age from thirteen to twenty, these kids had never been brought into the process of their own care, nor had they consequently begun any training to prepare them for eventually transitioning out of school and into the world.

After explaining why everyone was gathered, I made sure they all left that first meeting with a homework assignment: to ask their caregivers which of these three diagnoses they had.

To make a long story short, that particular support group succeeded because we then turned those sessions into a positively presented class about what we all had, going over all the characteristics in a nonnegative, sometimes humor-filled light. The students' participation grew as time went on, with raised hands and comments from all of them when they too shared the particular characteristic being discussed. Their relief was evident.

To their credit, the teachers who were observing this didn't cross their arms and become defensive. They instead uttered phrases like, "Oh my God, we never thought their knowing would make them feel like this. This is wonderful." These were *great* teachers.

Prior policies and legal issues perpetuated by antilabelism prevented these teachers from talking with their kids about diag-

In many instances, the parents of these kids were unaware of exactly what their child had. We have to remember that, for many people, such evaluations of their children are an economic impossibility. In situations where the diagnosis is unknown, tragic mistakes can follow, but not always. In many other instances, economically challenged communities learn to "get by" simply by adapting as best they can to the differences of their children who don't fit in. Economics rule our lives. There is no market for therapists, for instance, in developing third-world countries because nobody has the money to pay for what, to them, is a luxury item that as yet has no place in their culture. The problem here in the United States is that we could very well afford not to let these kids go undiagnosed, and subsequently slip through the cracks.

noses they'd already received (or in this case, that their parents had received regarding their children). However, other factors contributed. For one thing, these were inner-city kids from homes where economic realities had sometimes taken away much of their caregivers' abilities to partake in the culture of autism enlightenment, whether it be parent support groups or reading stacks of books.

In Our Own Voices

The seeds of where we are now began in the 1960s and 1970s, when autobiographical accounts written by people on the spectrum first surfaced. Books by Donna Williams, Thomas Mc-Kean, and Temple Grandin refuted the idea that autistic individuals were all incapable of communication, or of contributing insight into their own way of thinking. Adding to this wealth of information was the work of clinicians like Sacks, who brought attention to the beautiful work created by the autistic individuals he'd stumbled across in his studies. And in 1993, one year before AS was finally recognized and included in the *DSM-IV*, autistic Jim Sinclair wrote a landmark article titled "Don't Mourn for Us" that poignantly outlined a very real, though surprising conflict between the needs of suffering parents and the sometimes oppositional needs of the suffering autistic individual.

As the number of speakers on the spectrum grew, it started to become apparent that autism was complex enough that not one attitude, treatment, or strategy would work with everyone. People like Jerry Newport, Stephen Shore, and Liane Holliday Willey began to join the likes of Grandin and Williams on our bookshelves, and these new contributors were now writing more than just one "tell-all-now-I'll-disappear" book. Now they were writing second and third books, and subsequently their worth was becoming redefined. Suddenly it wasn't the experiences of people on the spectrum that were of importance and insight, it was also their *opinions*. They were figuratively moving from existing as zoo exhibits, to becoming *talking* zoo exhibits, and then to themselves becoming the zoologists. And the range of interpretations and suggested strategies, some written with fury, some with calm, also accurately dispelled the riduculous notion that there was only one, singular "face of autism."

What has also helped immensely are the scores of books diagnosing historically accomplished people with autism spectrum conditions. The following names are taken from only three books*

---

* *Asperger's Syndrome and High Achievement*, by Ioan James; *The Genius of Artistic Creativity*, by Michael Fitzgerald; and *Different Like Me*, by Jennifer Elder.

(there are more), and they can be thought of as constructive contributions to the psyche of the diagnosed individual: Albert Einstein, Isaac Newton, Henry Cavendish, Thomas Jefferson, Vincent van Gogh, Ludwig van Beethoven, Wolfgang Amadeus Mozart, Emily Dickinson, Ludwig Wittgenstein, Alan Turing, Hans Christian Anderson, Herman Melville, William Butler Yeats, Lewis Carroll, Arthur Conan Doyle, Erik Satie, Bela Bartok, George Orwell, Patricia Highsmith, Andy Warhol, Glenn Gould, Alfred Kinsey, Bertrand Russell, Immanuel Kant, Piet Mondrian, Wassily Kandinsky, Barbara McClintock, Paul Erdös, Nikola Tesla, Sophie Germain, Dian Fossey, Andy Kaufman, Julia Bowman Robinson, Joseph Cornell, and Benedict de Spinoza. Even if an individual hasn't a prayer of achieving similar accomplishments, knowledge of these revelatory associations can do wonders for an individual's self-esteem and capacity for hope.

The Tragic Story of Michael Bambrick

Michael Bambrick's story might sound unique, but as tragic as it is, it is not as unique as we might wish.

In 2006, GRASP started to receive checks in the mail attached to notes, letters, and Post-its on which was written, "In memory of Michael Bambrick." My heart sank, for I knew from experience what this meant. Upon investigation, I discovered that Michael Bambrick was a talented, handsome young man from Long Island, New York, in his mid-twenties, who could have soared to great heights in music, writing, or computer programming, yet chose to join the Air Force after the events of September 11. He had such difficulty processing his eventual diagnosis of AS that after a string of disappointments—leaving the Air Force, leaving another job after that, beginning a questionable new medication, experiencing a first case of heartbreak, and soon after the presence of the police in his home—Michael went to the local Home Depot, bought rope, walked into the woods near his home, and ended his life. In lieu of flowers, the family had asked for donations to be made to GRASP in his honor.

I visited the family shortly thereafter at their home and talked extensively with Michael's mother, Janet, and his only surviving sibling, Jill. I learned about a young man who had never been able to fit in, and who once had written his mother that his hope was to someday find people he could simply relate to. Overwhelmed with frustration, he had shut down. He had, in fact, metamorphosed into the euphemistic example described in the previous chapter, of the individual who sits in his room all day playing video games. He personified this stereotype to such an extent that he was involved in what's referred to as a "gaming community," where many people play each other online and talk between sessions. In one particular period, Michael was jobless, and owing to the all-night gaming, he was sleeping all day. When his mother threatened to turn the electricity off in his room, Michael responded, "Mom, this is the only community I've ever known. If you do that, I might as well slit my wrists." Whether this response was the product of despair or manipulation, he wasn't lying about it being the only community he'd ever known.

He was extremely depressed, yet according to his mother, he would not ask for help. "He was walking this fine line," his mother related, "between 'I'm stressed, and I need to be alone. But I'm lonely.'"

His mother also relayed another comment of Michael's, when a therapist asked him to describe his perfect world: "In my perfect world, someone would call me first." Yet his sister Jill quickly interjected, "But he wouldn't pick up the phone! We called him and he wouldn't pick up the phone!"

Extreme depression, rather than AS, drove Michael to cut his life short. But the social isolation and stigma caused by his AS had given birth to his depression.

Michael had come to our Long Island GRASP meeting once, but had been one of those not-so-infrequent people who was disturbed by those with greater challenges than he, if not by himself and his relationship to them. He never returned to a GRASP meeting as a result. And because we don't push people who seem hesitant to attend, we never pursued him. You hope for the best in those situations, and in Michael's case, the worst happened.

My friend Simon Harak, a Jesuit priest, once said to me: "The first step in life for anyone is to find a community." Simon's words have stayed with me more strongly since my own diagnosis. And a quote that indirectly argues against that idea, a quote that may stay with me equally, came from Michael's mother: "Do you know how many times in my life I've wished that I'd never mentioned the word *Asperger's* to him?"

If the negative stigma attached to the autism spectrum didn't exist, Michael would be looking at his social deficits without fear, thereby improving on them, and thereby letting the world in on his academic and creative abilities, still alive, and probably thriving.

"Happy and Sad at the Same Time"

GRASP member Jason Zervoudakes discovered AS on a diagnostic checklist posted on the Internet. Of his reaction, he wrote:

While reviewing it, tears came to my eyes. I was happy and sad at the same time. On the one hand, I felt relieved because I understood why most of my life was miserable. On the other hand, I felt bad because I was unwilling to get help for a long time.

Even in the most positive of circumstances surrounding when and how we find out, there will always be some negatives to temper the relief.

I personally came to this diagnosis through my then-four-year-old son, C.C. When C.C. was two, he began to exhibit many of the telltale signs that something was different. Speech and motor skills issues were compounded by an inability to play with other kids his age. But his differences were also displayed through a preference for organizing blocks, toys, and dog food cans into piles distinguished by color, shape, or size . . . rather than "playing" with them. Many people said, "Oh, boys are just delayed sometimes, that's all," but we knew something was up. And after a year or so of hearing tests, play therapy, and speech therapy, the word *Asperger's* was mentioned.

Because of the genetic nature of AS, the clinicians who were looking at C.C. were now also looking at me out of the corners of their eyes. One thing led to another, and in November 2000, C.C. and I were diagnosed within a week of each other.

Dr. Richard Perry, who diagnosed us both, urged me not to make too much of it. After all, I was on the very "higher-functioning" end of the autistic spectrum. But when I heard the diagnosis, a tidal wave instantly flooded me from the bottom up. I nearly fainted. Lifelong notions that maybe I thought differently from others . . . these were now confirmed.

Leading up to that day, I had welcomed the investigation.

Long before my appointment, even before my night in Cabo san Lucas, I sensed the release this particular diagnosis might bring me. So much of my thirty-six years of life had been eventful, but confusing and significantly unexplained. And were I to share this "ailment" with my son, it would then take away some of the fear I had of C.C. going through life, and the world, with such a potentially alienating distinction. If I had whatever C.C. had, if C.C. could be assisted through shared experience by someone who loved him as much as I loved C.C., then he might navigate through life more successfully. However bumpy the road might be for us both, I figured it was better than being lost.

As for me, I finally had answers to the myriad of events that had left me scratching my head over the years. Waking up in school from daydreams to find that a teacher was yelling at me, or that other kids were laughing at me, or that even sometimes people were applauding—this discovery, if I could handle it well, might bring wonderful closure to those mountains of confusion.

The internal pros tend to greatly outweigh the internal cons. But the cons exist, and need to be identified so that we can address them.

Those that stick out from having seen them repeatedly in GRASP's adult support groups (or from my having experienced them personally) are as follows:

1. The aforementioned stigma.

2. The realization that there has always been a gulf between you and your loved ones. For many people, this diagnosis confirms that there really was something separating you and the people you loved or spent time with, a division that many people, myself included, enjoyed pretending didn't exist. We may have long suspected that this gulf existed, but

we shook it off—"Nah, that couldn't be true"—because these were indeed our loved ones. Who wants to think that there's a barrier there?

3. The end of the dream that you will one day wake up and find that you are now just like everyone else. This is not a common scenario, but GRASP has seen it enough to warrant mention. Oddly enough, one's ability to join with the rest of the world is increased tenfold by now having the diagnosis. But for a few, this new information can feel very tragic.

4. The years that may, at first, appear to have been "wasted." The years trying to do things that others did instinctively. There will always be a sense of loss, however big or small. But the hard work that one may have spent forever trying to mirror everyone else can perhaps now seem remarkable, and a source of great pride if the individual has a strong work ethic. As Zervoudakes writes:

> What amazed me was how much I was able to achieve without knowing why I wasn't in sync with everyone else . . . I look back on what I achieved and say, "Wow! I don't know how I was able to do that."

5. Depression.

Depression

In what is admittedly testimonial evidence as opposed to clinically researched data, I have seen depression (or at least the feeling of being terribly overwhelmed) in almost everyone that goes through the diagnostic process. However, and this is a big "however," unless the person is willfully determined to be forever sad, or has accumulated as much disappointment as Michael Bambrick had, the depression goes away. In people who have never truly known real depression, it seems to last around two months. And in people who have had experience with depression, it seems to last around six months.

I myself had never known depression. I'd always been the happy type who was blessed with a confused but strong sense of self-worth. But when I got diagnosed, my anticipated glee at having such a huge weight lifted off my shoulders suddenly wasn't there. When I left the doctor's office that day, I was completely caught off guard by a wave of defeatist thought (I remember clearly being on the sidewalk, wondering what was happening to me). In that moment of diagnosis, the euphoria I'd predicted and started to feel was quickly metamorphosing into a fast-moving hurricane of unstoppable negativity—a monumental sadness with the realization that, "Yes, you *were* all alone your whole life! You do *not* belong in the same category as these other people! You do *not* (as you suspected somewhere in your recesses) have that sense of shared experience . . . with anyone!" My reaction admittedly went too far into the irrational, yet I know now that this was probably a very necessary part of the process for me. All the personality quirks of mine that had been chalked up either to weirdness, to artistic eccentricity, or to a truly unique personality were now lumped into the cold, stigmatizing mark of something broken. And within this new context I was typical. Under the light of AS, I was really nobody special.

These cons, these feelings from within, are hard, but they go away—far, far away if you make an effort to process what all this means to you. The positive changes my diagnosis has brought me in the years since have obliterated those negative feelings. Promise.

A Quick Note on Gender

Past studies have shown ratios around 5 to 1 or 4 to 1 in favor of males being diagnosed on the spectrum over females. However, given how badly we have been at seeing the diagnosis in females, these studies are suspect, and in the future risk being completely invalidated. Whether the ratio is actually 50–50 or not, boys with AS are identified more easily because gender expectations are so different. Boys are more expected to make eye contact whereas it's more okay for girls to appear "shy." Boys are more expected to join in on team sports whereas girls are predominantly not. Submissive women in abusive relationships are looked down upon or pitied, but are not a cause for neurological concern, whereas submissive men are (and have a much harder time entering relationships at all, thus increasing the chances that people will notice their differences) . . . The list of parallel inconsistencies goes on.

An autism spectrum diagnosis still does not dictate everything about you. In addition to your neurological makeup, you are the product of the culture in which you live, of your gender, of your race, of your economic background, of your sexual orientation, and of the quality of the support systems you've either enjoyed or been subject to. One of C.C.'s classmates, for example, was a three-year-old girl named Lin. She came from a Chinese family, and went to a Chinese-speaking school in Chinatown. And when Lin's parents got the AS diagnosis, they accordingly took their daughter out of the Chinese school to get her into a specialized program to meet her diagnostic needs. The school officials, however, berated the parents with cries of "How can you do this?"

To them, a girl who sat quietly by herself, reading books, and who didn't want anything to do with peers or noisy play . . . this was the perfect little girl.

Many would argue that girls are luckier in that they get away with these traits, yet the truth lies in the opposite. Girls have it worse because they are at much greater risk for never getting the diagnosis that can so richly improve their lives.

Additional Cons, or "Obstacles"

"The Cowboy Culture"

Our culture, like Chinese culture, like all cultures, has pros and cons. The first obstacle has to do with what I refer to as "The Cowboy Culture," a way of thinking that is not restricted to just Americans.

"Ah, you're just making excuses."

"Oh, hopping on the latest psychiatric fad, this 'Asperger's syndrome.'"

"You just want attention. Work your problems out yourself."

"Everyone has problems."

"*Now* what's wrong with you?"

That most of these reactions are the consequence of ignorance or frustration should be a given, for the conveyors of these attitudes would think differently if they knew anything about the autism spectrum. But ignorant or not, they cause damage. Their attitudes are unknowingly invalidating the very real experiences of the individual with AS. Even when we, the recipients of the diagnosis, are armed with the knowledge that such words are nonsense, the words still hurt. And they hurt not only because these words usually come from people close to us, but also because they are words that may reflect the culture we've been raised in—that a part of *us* believes in as well.

In truth, this is a culture that does more service than disservice. For it *would* be wrong for someone to let his or her diagnosis become an excuse, or to let it encourage a lifelong pursuit of victimization, as some people have indeed done. But it is imperative that diagnosed individuals rebuff these words, and instead examine all the items that are put in front of them when they're diagnosed—the items about their family, about their past. It is hard to see at that moment of being criticized, but the real cowardice is to bury this diagnosis as if it meant nothing.

Until the messengers of these hurtful words gain more knowledge, the diagnosed individual should not rely on them to be a source of support. These are often people we love, so we can't just dismiss them, but we have to walk away to some degree. We have enough work ahead of us without vainly trying to change others.

I'll never know whether Michael Bambrick said to himself, "I'll just deal with it," in reference to his diagnosis. But I've heard others utter these words, walking away from me, or from a support group, rushing out the door, desperate to get away. These situations don't turn out well. They don't always end as Michael Bambrick's story ended, but the individual who refuses to examine the consequences of the diagnosis usually doesn't "deal" at all. He instead runs, and that person will have a lasting cloud hanging over him.

Many of my family members wanted me to either downplay the diagnosis or keep it secret. I didn't tell many that I had an upcoming diagnostic appointment, but those that I told not only believed I wouldn't be given the diagnosis, they just flat out didn't want it. We have to remember that because of the genetics involved, and because of the new interpretations of the past that will have to be explored, we are not the only ones affected by our diagnosis. When we make the decision to seek a diagnosis, we inadvertently put a lot of work on the plate of family members who may not have asked for that work, who may not have appreciated our decision to go get checked out, and who may be petrified of what it might say about *them*.

The following is important: They will have their own walk to walk when you get diagnosed. But that is *their* walk, not yours. And unlike your decision to walk your walk, they may choose to avoid theirs. This is something you can do little about. The shared love among you may entice you to try and change them, but you can only do so much, even though it's painful to watch as a loved one avoids their walk.

The cowboy act oddly shows itself to be the cowardly response. Your decision to face all this (though motivated by obvious self-interest given how much you'll gain) is very brave. *You're* the courageous one here, specifically *because* you'll be going against the grains of vastly differing ideas about what courage really is.

———————

THE night after my diagnosis I sat on the edge of my son C.C.'s bed at around 2 a.m. He'd customarily kicked his covers off and, as usual, was sprawled across the bed. I looked hard at him, and staring at his sleeping face, I debated. I didn't have to be public about the fact that I had AS. I could instead suck it up, if I wanted, and avoid what could probably be months of attention to the self that would leave me very vulnerable to criticism. I could just forget about my diagnosis, and just deal with C.C.'s needs, as most of my family and friends wanted me to. These were the rules we'd all previously lived by, and like the rest of the world, my loved ones sought likenesses in those close to them, not differences.

My decision was reached the next day. In an elevator ride with a coworker, I was asked how I was, and I shared C.C.'s diagnosis.

"Isn't that genetic?" she responded. And I—completely caught off guard again—petrified and defensive, spat out words like: "Oh, no. I don't think so. Not really . . ."

As the elevator doors opened, I felt like I had stabbed my own son in the back. What garbage it would be for me to say to him later on that he had nothing to be ashamed about when I was experiencing such obvious shame . . . Paying little attention to my diagnosis was *not* dealing with C.C.'s needs whatsoever. I would, in fact, be hurting him.

Opening Up to Change

The phrase "opportunity for change" sounds great; but one of the diagnostic criteria's highlighted points is "doesn't like breaks in routine." Probably no one likes change, even if the distaste is felt more by individuals on the spectrum. When someone senses there are huge changes coming to his or her life, too often even the positive alterations will be abandoned out of that fear of change itself.

But when we see an improvement to our lives due to one change, we become less afraid to make other changes. Soon after my diagnosis, for instance, I realized how unhappy I was continuing with a "starving artist" theatre career, when fatherhood created the need to make more money. Yet I had sworn all my life that theatre was where I belonged. Colleagues argued with me: "Stick it out, it takes a long time." But I did it. I quit theatre. That was a huge change that I was aching to make, and it was made easier thanks to all the change I'd endured in getting diagnosed with AS.

I made another huge change . . . To many people, my first

wife and I were the perfect couple. We got along, but we were not happy. We amicably agreed to divorce five months after my diagnosis based not on a failed marriage, but on the realization that the marriage had been a mistake from the beginning; what we had was an arrangement based on friendship and mutual admiration, not on (what I now know to be) love. Both of our beliefs in the sanctity of marriage were high, but being happy was, and is, more important. Does a divorce on my résumé still feel like a stain, and a failure? Yes. But the ability to admit the failure was key to moving on.

Individualized Therapy

Support groups such as those organized by GRASP can help immensely in coming to terms with the diagnosis. But GRASP groups are not everywhere (yet!), and they are not meant to be a substitute for individualized therapy. You might have the healthiest possible outlook on your diagnosis, yet you might still benefit from one-on-one counseling.

GRASP groups thrive on the trust that peer-run shared experience can bring about, for most individuals spend their lives trying to explain themselves to those who are supposedly in charge of their care, often failing, and often withdrawing further as a result of accumulated failure. There may have been plenty of instances where well-meaning figures in our lives asked for our trust, but hadn't earned it according to our standards (as opposed to *their* standards). We may have been in error not to trust them, but if they didn't display a capacity to understand us, then we most likely could not share with them. And in some cases this may have even been quite wise. Through your distrust you might have been protecting already wounded feelings.

Do your research in finding an appropriate therapist. Not everyone who professes to be comfortable in treating individuals with AS is actually qualified. Obtaining therapist recommendations from local autism centers, support groups, and other resources available to you is strongly recommended.

If you already have a therapist that you like at the time of diagnosis, yet realize that his or her knowledge of the spectrum is limited, then you should strongly consider switching to someone else. This can be painful, and can leave you feeling like you're losing a great friend. But it's not your responsibility to pay a therapist to learn about AS. And someone who would take your money in such a situation is no friend of yours.

In these support groups, the rush of shared experience can be immense, and there is nothing like that first realization that you are not alone. But sometimes those good feelings trick us into thinking we have no need for individualized therapy. Quite the contrary. One-on-one sessions with a qualified professional who is familiar with the autism spectrum can be immensely helpful.

Self-Diagnosis

Self-diagnosis isn't just when the individual figures out for himself that he has AS. It's a term now, a colloquial phrase that many people use (as in "I'm self-diagnosed") to convey that they have little or no intention of getting a formal diagnosis, if only to prove that which they already know.

In the support groups I ran, I used to say:

"Yes, 99.9 percent of those of you who are self-diagnosed are usually right. When something hits you like a ton of bricks as you read about AS and you internally shout, 'That's it!' . . . then you're usually on the right track."

GRASP's Robert Hedin, who runs our Philadelphia network, is a prime example of someone self-diagnosed who is thriving. He defies the idea that self-diagnosis is unadvisable based on the dignity and self-assurance with which he seems to walk every step of his life. But Bob, I have come to realize, is the exception, and not the rule. My opinion toward self-diagnosis has changed over the years, and I now recommend the clinician's confirming stamp very highly.

My opinion about the accuracy rate hasn't changed whatsoever. But whereas I empathized with the need to save the money that a clinical diagnosis usually requires, I started to see a disturbing pattern in some self-diagnosed folks: I began to hear stronger-than-usual complaints that they were feeling doubt from the world that they could actually be on the spectrum. Some even complained that the doubt came from me. I was confused. I'd always conveyed the "99.9 percent . . ." statement to them, and so I was puzzled as to how they might have misinterpreted me. This imaginary criticism, often irreversible despite reassurances to the contrary, led me to believe that with self-diagnosis there is still going to be some measure of *internal* doubt.

I could sympathize. I know that with all the doubt there was from people I love, that I needed that official diagnosis in order to withstand the pressure to shrug off my AS as nonsense. (I, in fact, got a second opinion confirming the diagnosis once I decided to work in this field, proving that on an internal level, I really needed the outside confirmation.) I know that my family and friends never would have adjusted to the idea that I did indeed have AS unless it came from a trained doctor, and that "proof" has made my life decidedly easier. Furthermore, it has made the lives of family and friends easier as well. With their varying feelings of disbelief now educated, they can focus more on exploring what my diagnosis means to *them*.

For many people, not having an official diagnosis can prevent them from having the conviction to be able to move forward. Very few people, for instance, go out and spend hard-earned money on books about AS with the same drive as someone who *knows* they have AS. That alone is reason to get a clinician's opinion.

Are there no pretenders then? Aren't there some who actually don't have AS, but who say they do? Yes, and these are sad, sad situations. For these are usually cases where the real diagnosis carries much worse stigma than AS, and where medications are more necessary both in quantity and quality. When they avoid the more severe stigma, and jump on an imaginary AS bandwagon, the person never gets treated for what they have and tough times inevitably follow.

Even with the diagnosis, most people will still carry the fear that they won't be believed. We get this piece of paper, this confirmation, in order to have our experiences finally justified or understood. And whereas the internal reaction of "that's it!" is real when we first read a description of AS, like it or not, we are affected by the outside world's reaction to our diagnosis. If we're going to live among them, then we need them to validate what we've gone through.

Keeping a Journal or Diary

What a confirmation it was for me read in the memoirs of Dawn Prince-Hughes and Liane Holliday Willey that they had benefited greatly by keeping diaries after being diagnosed. I had done the same, and they corroborated my feeling that this had done me a world of good.

For four and a half months after my diagnosis, I also kept a diary, noting all the changes I went through as I processed all the information that was coming to me. I told no one, absolutely no one, that I was keeping this journal, not even my wife. Because to have a place to discuss what were *my* thoughts as I endured the thoughts and opinions of others—this allowed me to feel as though I had a place to go, to be honest, where I didn't have to take care of anyone other than myself, and where the sanctity and weight of this unbelievable process would never come into question.

Whatever the individual may think of his or her writing ability (frankly, my journal was mostly charts and notes rather than prose), this is a fool-proof, no-brainer piece of advice. Keep a journal. For one thing, meeting these challenges isn't just empowering, or gratifying; it's also fascinating.

Conclusion

Wherever you find yourself at this moment, having concrete reasons to explain the mysteries of what once was, reasons that have nothing to do with personal defect . . . this should be a blessing. It wasn't *you*.

Most of the time, the diagnosis won't be what floors you. The "label" is still something that some of us can choose not to disclose. Individuals who are more equipped to mirror others have the option of revealing their diagnosis to no one; and those that are not as well equipped can choose to leave their differences undefined (a subject called "Disclosure," which we'll cover later).

But a word of caution: If we all concealed our diagnosis, would life then go on as it always has? No. Again, our behavioral differences are what set us apart, not the label. And what is truly overwhelming is the flood of new information the diagnosis brings—the new interpretations not only about yourself, but also about the people around you.

This is not bad news, this is good news. Maybe the best you've ever had.

CHAPTER THREE

Long Walks: Looking Back on the Past with a New Perspective

He who seeks revenge digs two graves.
—Old Chinese Proverb

———————

STRANGELY enough, in the writings of recently diagnosed people, I have seen the same three-word sentence many times:

"No one knew."

Does this mean that multiple authors are plagiarizing one another? No. What's happening to those lucky writers is that these three words are simply appearing, somehow, some way, as a gift from their minds or their hearts (you can almost see the lightbulb above their heads as they wrote). Linguistically, it is the perfect embodiment of how to process all the missteps that may have gone before.

———————

IN the last chapter I talked about "walking your walk." I meant it literally *and* figuratively.

The day after I was diagnosed, I stumbled upon the "walk your walk" remedy by accident. My son loved the Brooklyn Botanical Gardens. And since the gardens were right around the corner from our apartment, we went frequently. He meticulously loved to trace one of the garden streams, following the water's path that ran through the mile-wide landscape from one end to the other. Now in a stage where he was attaching words to visual images (he had earlier memorized the entire *Audubon Field Book of Mushrooms*), he was currently asking to have the names of every plant read to him. Diagnosed less than twenty-four hours earlier, I needed a breather, so when he asked if we could go that day, I jumped at the chance.

To say that this particular walk was cathartic would be a gross underestimate. I'd struck gold. Once there, I immediately felt much more able to face the ramifications of the diagnosis. Long walks in these gardens would be my path away from feeling overwhelmed.

So C.C. and I went every day, ten days in a row, to what for me was the healthiest arena possible to revisit the past, to try and finally piece together the puzzle that had been "thus far." Within these gardens I felt safe. I felt as though I had been transported by Divine Providence into an atmosphere wherein I could finally stop my perpetual motion of thirty-six years, of moving past confusing episodes, and where I could finally dare to look back.

For one thing, having C.C. there prevented me from giving in to the sadness of loss—the loss of wasted efforts when I thought I was someone I was not—for fatherhood means it's not all about you anymore. *Feel* the loss? Yes. But because of C.C. I could not collapse from it, and I had to learn from it. Furthermore, the reassurance of flowers, and trees, and fish, gave me the sense that everything grows, and changes, uninterrupted despite what had happened to me. All would eventually be okay. Lastly, these were mild November days when few people visit the gardens. So I had plenty of room to breathe, or to stop and gasp at a memory without feeling self-conscious.

Somewhat strategically, somewhat unconsciously, I put together the pieces of all that my diagnosis was providing me: about my family, my schooling, my relationships, and my careers. For prior to my diagnosis I had not been aware that I had studied other people's facial expressions in order to copy them, or that I had looked for what people *wanted to hear* after realizing that I didn't intuitively understand what they were trying to communicate. My mind raced back, and I saw places and instances where my social inabilities had hampered my progress in life—minor time bombs of discomfort that I planted in people who could have helped me.

At the time I thought these walks, this process, was the most remarkable thing anyone had ever gone through. And yet in listening to scores of other people's stories through GRASP, as I would do in the years that followed, I discovered how common my process had been. This discovery phase, as I would later learn, is not unique. Wonderful, but not rare. And there may be hundreds of thousands, if not more, who will undergo it in the years that follow today—the hardest and most beautiful walks I may ever walk.

Almost every memorable occurrence in one's life gets reevaluated under this new light. The post-diagnosis revelations place the individual in a new world, with new interpretations to nearly everything that has gone on before, where prior heroes might not appear so heroic anymore, or where past slights are revealed for not having been slights at all.

And it doesn't stop there. I write this six years after my diagnosis, and I still often stop dead in the street, suddenly hit by the realization that some past incident hadn't gone the way I'd originally interpreted. When you take the time to truly investigate all that the diagnosis can imply, you may find ways in which you successfully accrued masking strategies to get by. You may find hurtful moments that you'd buried so that you would be able to move past them. You may find areas where, in order to get by, you believed everything wrong that the world believed about you. You may find embarrassing areas where your own frustrations were displayed inappropriately thanks to how little you yourself knew about where the frustrations were coming from. You may discover that, in order to navigate the pressure to conform, you succeeded more through anthropologically sewn costumes than through sameness.

In this chapter—appropriately the longest chapter of the book—we'll go over the long list of possible discoveries awaiting you. No one will identify with everything discussed—as stated prior, this is not a cookie-cutter syndrome—but it may be helpful to examine those areas where you *didn't* experience similar roads in order to understand the scope of the diagnosis you now share with others.

THE concept of "No one knew" can also be taken further. Strung together, these three words serve as our generalized forgiveness of the world. But this sense of forgiveness will prove useful if applied to specific memories as well. For as you rehash the life you have lived, and reacquaint yourself with the people in your past who intentionally or unintentionally may have hurt you, notions of forgiveness will more than help. Forgiveness, by definition—in both the world's religious, and secularist, theories—doesn't imply that we have to *like* the people that once made our lives hard. And it certainly doesn't mean we have to want to spend time with these people—quite frankly, this is rarely a good idea. But the anger towards them hurts only us. Forgiving these tormentors is easier said than done, I know, and it is especially hard to forgive those who are close to us, like family. We expose more of our weak spots to such people; so when they hurt us, the perceived betrayal of trust and vulnerability makes things hurt more.

But for our own sake, we have to try. If this act, if this extension of "No one knew," can't happen today, then you should work to have it happen someday. Because forgiveness doesn't free past perpetrators. It frees you.

Family

As you begin to scan back through your memories, you may encounter prior jobs, university experiences, caregivers, boyfriends and girlfriends, and so forth that all require reevaluation. But our family life is the constant that we most likely still grapple with today. Families, after all, never stop existing. Cultural factors, economic factors, sibling issues, and many other filters will determine how your family handled you. Some families coped very well with their "different kid," and some didn't. Many protected their unusual children from the wrath of an outside world that didn't understand them; and many didn't. And in a cruel twist of fate, families that do the best job protecting the child are often the ones that have the hardest time letting go when it becomes time.

Without love from a supportive family, we often don't land on our own two feet when life throws a punch. But accumulated frustrations within the family dynamic (caused mostly by not knowing about the diagnosis) can significantly hide that love, a love that exists but that may have gotten mired in confusion the same way a car gets stuck in the mud. In countless GRASP support groups, there is often resentment displayed toward family members—especially parents. Such emotions have to be vented in order to validate the hurtful acts and words of frustration that may have followed both sides' inability to understand your AS. These are productive feelings, but only as a stepping stone toward acceptance.

Writing in the book *Voices from the Spectrum*, Beth Adler, in her essay "No! You Don't Understand," writes of a heartbreaking childhood:

Why did covering my ears make you so uncomfortable? . . . Mom. Dad. You've been gone a long time now. I know how much you loved me, but what I remember most about my childhood was you two yelling at me all the time. 'Why do you keep whining like that?' . . . Your angry faces scared me, and the sound of your yelling was so painful I had to whine to drown it out.

Even bestselling author Donna Williams writes:

My mother's response was to drive me, and all my belongings, to an aunt to try and give me away. My aunt wouldn't take me.

In lesser cases, where serious detachment did not occur among family members (and which are thankfully more frequent), cognitive awareness of why things transpired will resolve hurt feelings. GRASP member Gregory H. Gorski, writing about his relationship with his father, provides one such example:

> [My father] was, back then, still under the delusion that I could be good at sports if I tried harder, despite the fact that I had never been good at them and had no desire to even try. My mom and I wanted him to read the book on Asperger's, which he put off for months in a state of denial. He would not accept that something was "wrong" with his darling child. Eventually, after months of pressure, he very slowly read the book. I suppose that, over time, he came to not see it as something wrong, but just as something different. Perhaps he even saw a bit of himself in the book's descriptions. He eventually became supportive, and dropped those delusions of me being an athlete.

A controversial idea that we have presented in our groups is that it may be unfair for us to be mad at these loved ones for not understanding us. Master's degrees in neuroscience, after all, did not accompany our birth certificates. Not all of us come from parents who enjoyed educational opportunities. Some of us may also come from families too overwhelmed by their own lives to properly cope with behavioral and cognitive differences in their child. In larger families, the now-diagnosed individual may not have enjoyed the percentage of their parents' time that might have helped. Families living in rural communities too are somewhat handicapped because they are usually the last to reap the benefits of any new developments in sociological thinking. And lastly, AS's late inclusion into the pantheon of diagnoses figures highly in our families' capacity for ineffectiveness (for no one knew). These ideas are not controversial because they might offend you, the diagnosed individual. For once explained, the ideas might make sense as to *why* your family was unable to understand you. But they are ideas that are very hard for family members, especially parents, to swallow. Despite the legitimate alibi that the above rationale provides them for their mistakes, they are often deeply offended by the suggestion that they might not have understood their children.

The measuring stick, or what we should expect, as we look back to judge our families, is that they tried. In many cases, they may have not. The parents may have given up too early for you to feel comforted. But in most cases, the individual looking back should be able to find instances where the attempt was decidedly made, even if it ended in failure. Repeated failures, you could argue, are the mark of exemplary parents because they kept trying.

Other family members figure in as well. Grandparents often feel they had to care for two generations when a child was on the spectrum. And the household dynamic may have also included sibling difficulties where, if you were fairly challenged, you thus required more of your parents' time or resources. In such cases, the family atmosphere may have left both you *and* your neurotypical (NT)* sibling feeling neglected. These NT siblings may have been told they were lucky (compared to you), and thought to themselves, "How am I lucky when I get a fraction of the time my challenged brother [or sister] gets?" Siblings too will have their own walk to walk when the diagnosis is presented.

Neurotypical, or NT for short, refers to people who are not on the autism spectrum. The word is not intended (nor usually received) as a derogatory term, but the only remaining option used to indicate the greater majority is the word *normal*, which indicates that we are *abnormal*, and which further threatens already vulnerable self-esteem. Furthermore, the word *normal* also insults neurotypicals, who are just as unique as individuals as we are. Most of them rightfully object to the term *normal* as much as we would *abnormal*.

The family's pressure to conform, just like the diagnosed individual's, will have played a role as well, for if there is one constant among all families in this situation, it is that they needed the strength to defend their child during the more vulnerable younger years against that not-so-understanding world. Every parent will have endured pressure from schools, neighborhoods, places of worship; and even from extended family, to "change that child."

I, for instance, could not wear ties as a child. Ties, and the top button of dress shirts, made me feel a burning sensation around my neck and sent me into a panic. This posed a problem during formal family occasions when my cousins would be dressed up yet I wasn't. I also didn't eat vegetables other than corn, onions, and lettuce. The texture, taste, and smell of other vegetables triggered a gag reflex in me.* My mother (a single parent, and therefore susceptible to enough criticism as it was) was inaccurately thought of as a deficient caregiver, and I was inaccurately portrayed as a brat.

Other families may have teased the child for their differences, and treated them with what will now, looking back, feel like insulting condescension. The condescension will have to stop in the future, if it hasn't already. But you must understand that, in these instances, your families could have performed far worse. Given societal pressure to conform, condescension was probably the best response to your differences, at the time, that they could summon.

Some other families found it easy to take pride in a child who was mysteriously different, so long as there were enough special abilities, or positively perceived qualities, to compensate. And in the case of AS, this is frequently the case.

---

*Go figure: I've been fine with ties and vegetables since I was in my twenties, possibly because I cognitively began to understand my need for them as I grew older.

As in all the facets of this looking-back process—school, bullying, jobs—there may be incidents of great trauma to be reappraised. But as hard as it is to fathom, we must someday come to terms with the idea that our differences, in a world that didn't understand us, placed a burden on the family dynamic, even if we *ourselves* did not. In almost every individual's travels into this past dynamic, there is bound to be the need for varying degrees of healing.

In more serious cases, apologies may be necessary. One young man, diagnosed at age twenty-four, could not survive a single GRASP support group without passionately expressing anger toward his parents, or for the world that would not employ him or provide him with companionship. It's one thing to do this at one meeting, but it's another thing to repeat the tirade at subsequent meetings. He'd had a truly rough time. He had been mistakenly institutionalized by his parents in a residential psychiatric hospital when he was thirteen, and he stayed there for years, not only enduring the debilitating atmosphere and the loss of developmentally appropriate experiences, but also becoming harmed by misprescribed antipsychotic pharmaceuticals that contained damaging short- and long-term side effects. Now correctly diagnosed, but unable to handle all the mistakes that had transpired in the past, he was uncontrollably mired in anger. The rest of this particular GRASP group appealed to his very evident intellectual abilities, as well as to his particular faith (he was a very religious person) that he needed to let much of this go.

One day I got a call from his mother, which led to two more calls. And because the group was not reaching her son, I asked that she and her husband apologize to the young man for the lost years. I related that while such an idea might seem silly, even perhaps condescending to them, their son needed it. Aghast, though not angry with me, the mother exploded, relating to me the story of when he had gone after her with a knife, an act which precip-itated his institutionalization. Understanding her dilemma, and possible blamelessness, I still reiterated my request—they needed to forgive *him*. And I lobbied that her son's need in this instance was more important than their indignation.

She eventually told me that her husband refused the idea. The young man gradually disappeared after an outburst or two and we haven't heard from him since.

Few recently diagnosed individuals will identify with such a story. But if you can hear it, and allow such a worst-case scenario to temper the justifiably ill feelings that will surface as you walk your walks, then your own journey toward closure will be made easier.

School

When I was growing up, other kids would call me a retard. I hap-pen to be an incredibly intelligent and very articulate person. But I never did well in school. My social skills were horrible up until my mid 20's when I began to show some improvement.

—GRASP member Paul F. Miller III

Whereas the sense of betrayal often felt in difficult family situa-tions can tear us apart with its never-ending permanence, at least we get to leave school. Yet the social minefield that is the school experience can be a different source of lingering bitterness be-cause the difficulties are rarely resolved before the student leaves. And we can't go back. Difficult memories may therefore still burn inside the recently diagnosed adult.

We don't go to school simply for academic development. We also attend in order to develop socially. We go to be with peers in a supervised setting so as to learn to communicate, to gain social skills, and to have the same age-appropriate experiences in a collective, supposedly safe environment. But due to different logical wiring or the disadvantage toward nonverbal communication, the undiagnosed student with AS will have had a disproportionately harder time during these years. The social world can be excruciatingly difficult to navigate, and such uncharted territory isn't confined to just the other students: As well as playground and classroom issues with peers, there are almost always difficulties with teachers as well, especially in a situation where the student is wrongly presumed to be neurotypical. For when a child on the spectrum doesn't respond to the same treatment that others respond to, many teachers, especially if they've never heard of AS, will make mistakes.

This long period in our lives is often the one most filled with embarrassing moments. This may be true for everyone, NTs as well as those on the spectrum, but it's especially true for the undiagnosed child with AS. School is often where we first suspected that we were different. It is where we often begin a process of resigning our lives to being comparatively friendless, and it is also where we perhaps learned to be distrustful—even disrespectful—of authority figures.

Most people on the spectrum internalize. Whether we are aware or not of certain emotions, people with AS divulge those emotions less because we either didn't recognize them, or we sensed during school years that those in charge of our care didn't "get" us. It is difficult for anyone, on the spectrum or not, to reveal such private information to people they do not trust.

There are good school experiences out there as well, and I enjoyed three great years in school after nine relatively lousy ones. The change occurred because I switched schools; moving from an elite school to an alternative school that proved to be a more welcoming, stimulating environment for me.

My mother taught eighth graders at an influential Providence, Rhode Island, school for girls. As a benefit, she received free tuition for me to attend Providence's influential school for boys. From first until ninth grade, I instead endured countless problems at this school. My behavioral differences were quickly interpreted as indicative of a troublemaker. And the subsequent frustrations that *both* the teachers and I had with one another further deteriorated relationships that had already been destroyed.

Finally, when I was fifteen, after nearly being kicked out numerous times over the years, I left, and began attending an experimental school called "School One." School One had no proms, no yearbooks, no sports, and an open mind. Instead of ivy-covered brick walls centered in a well-groomed campus, It was in a converted downtown bowling alley. Suddenly I wasn't the suspected drug addict who went out of his way to disrupt classes. I was now thought of as talented. Academically and socially, the positive change was overnight. And the relief I felt at having a change of scenery and a clean slate was near-biblical. I was in heaven.

Even in positive school environments, there are still lessons to be learned; about understanding social rank, about understanding deception or manipulation (often a negative word for *navigation*—the day I first noticed C.C. trying to manipulate me, I jumped for joy). And in varying degrees of severity, there are sensory challenges to overcome. Loud bells, fluorescent lights, the cacophony of students and their voices filling the halls; all this can deepen the AS child's need for quiet moments of solitude, moments that are sometimes available only in bath-room stalls.

Adding to this can be the stress of not knowing why all this bothers you, but doesn't seem to bother anyone else. Our in-ability to express—or trust enough to express—our anxieties and confusion is usually the recipe for so-called behavioral problems, and can lead to the oft-heard "If that was my kid, why, I'd . . . " Even in instances where we are showered with praise, often there is the sense that the one praising is operating under a misassumption. A better problem to have, no doubt, but this still adds to the individual's uncertain feelings about the world around him.

Academic Mishandling

In general, the individual on the spectrum is quite intelligent, and many students may have breezed through their coursework. This is oddly enough often a great disadvantage. For in many cases the student was never challenged or given work appropriate to her abilities. The casualty is the student's work ethic. By think-ing she worked hard because she got an "A," the distinction be-tween talent and effort is often never identified.

But there are also many instances in our past where there were academic failures, through an inability, for example, to focus on something we are not interested in. This affects the social sphere too, as this inability, like many other AS qualities, unfairly la-beled us as disrespectful and rebellious. Also, our interest level alone doesn't dictate whether or not the grades will be high. Even in subjects of interest, there can be obstacles where an AS way of thinking collides with strategies that don't accommodate it. One example still in practice today, even with identified kids on the spectrum—is the practice of proving your work in math class.

Many individuals on the spectrum (including my son and I) often breezed through many a math class, until that year arrived when they were made to prove their work. This can have negative results for the individual on the spectrum for two reasons:

- Because we often process this type of information faster, our computations are harder to see, to visualize, and therefore to put on paper. Imagine trying to spot a license plate on a car going eighty miles per hour versus a car going twenty miles per hour. One is easier than the other. If the answers came to us slower, we'd have enough time to be able to see how we arrived at them.

- Often in these classes, teachers will also encourage the student to arrive at the correct conclusion via different means. In other words, even proving how you arrived at your conclusion isn't enough. Certain curriculums believe in a "my way or the highway" formula in which kids are expected to arrive at mathematical answers, and this can have a disastrous effect on children with AS, not only frustrating them academically, but overwhelming them with unneeded frustration. It took enough effort to catch up with their thoughts, and now they need to come up with another solution? This makes no sense to the individual with AS, and the long-term damage is that it can discourage the student away from an area where there is great ability.

Limitations and/or restrictions are oddly enough often very helpful. For while words like *discipline* and *punishment* are usually associated negatively with structured, rule-based upbringings, the fact is that kids with AS feel safer in environments that are more clearly communicated. In creative writing classes, for instance, an initial panic might occur if a teacher places an empty sheet of paper in front of the student with the instruction, "Write whatever you want." Unless he comes to class with a clear (conscious or unconscious) idea of what he wants to write about, assignments like "Character A wants something from Character B. Set it at a fruit stand" will always provide a process for the student that feels safer. Fewer rules leave more to interpret, possibly causing the child with AS to feel uncertain within them.

But the *manner* in which instructions are given is of additional importance. Most of us take things very literally, and the more exact an instruction, the better off we will be (though too much instruction may come off as insulting), depending on the child's place on the spectrum.

Individuals on the spectrum can also go both ways in focusing more on details and less on the "big picture," or vice versa. And there may be social difficulty in play as the teacher may not understand the student's inability to complete the assignment to their satisfaction. Many individuals on the spectrum can think of vast worlds on their own. French autistic Gilles Tréhin spent twenty years designing his own city, the drawings of which are reflected in his book, *Urville*. Yet perhaps the majority of individuals on the spectrum provide detail after detail with no larger context, or as Roger Meyer, in his essay "The Way We Think" (published in the book *Voices from the Spectrum*), states so beautifully:

I have trouble seeing the forest because the trees are so interesting.

Any difficulties with academics may also have been emphasized as greater failures than they really were. Some children with AS, for example, perform very well on standardized tests used to determine natural intelligence. Why this doesn't translate onto a final exam will likely be misread as laziness or willful negligence. Even an enhanced ability with spoken language can be deceiving.

When I speak, for instance, my vocabulary is quite good, and I know how to construct a verbal sentence. But this is partially my AS at work, my "little professor syndrome." I'm not dumb, don't get me wrong, but I'm not as intelligent as I may sound in person.

Teacher Mistakes

Not knowing his student is different, or why she's different, causes many a teacher to make errors when judging either the student's motives, or in assessing what will resolve her challenges or anxiety. In the cases of best intentions, harm is still very possible. For example, even many years later, you might bristle at the phrase "Just be yourself" because of the memories it evokes (even though it likely came from those who wished you well). It stings because you knew that by doing exactly that, by "being yourself," there were often miserable consequences. Claire Sainsbury, who wrote a wonderful book about the AS child in the mainstream school experience, *Martian in the Playground*, compiled a list of such expressions that rarely worked when applied:

Everybody feels like that sometime.
You can do it if you just try.
I'm sure they like you really.
It's just a friendly teasing.

Just be yourself and everything will be fine.
There's nothing the matter with you.

Teachers may have failed to understand how exhausting recess periods could be. They may have misinterpreted the intense special interests of children with AS as pathological obsessions (the negative term for *passions*), and without understanding the damage they were doing, may have discouraged the student's participation in them. Teachers also may have mistaken attention issues, and fidgety behavior (rocking, or mild stimming) as stubbornness. These issues are sometimes addressed pharmaceutically, though many adults on the spectrum had these issues go away mysteriously as they learned to bury themselves in their work.

And then there are the situations where the good intentions from teachers either evaporated, or were never there to begin with; where any and all academic or social inabilities were seen as pure disobedience. I endured nine years of these interpretations. Granted, the disobedience became very real over time, as I became equally frustrated with them. But knowing where that disrespect came from, thanks to my diagnosis, helped immensely in finally being able to make sense of those years.

I was lucky. I still had some of those angry school reports. On my ten days of walks with C.C. I brought along the report cards I'd managed to find from seventh to ninth grades, my last years at that elite yet inappropriate school (earlier report cards had sadly not been saved). I was glad I had them, yet I was petrified to read them. I'd been extremely happy every year of my life since those nine years. And even amid the strength of self-assuredness, of a present confidence brought to fruition by a life sprinkled with enough success to sustain me, I still didn't want to read those old report cards because of the memories they might summon. But smelling the release they might add to those walks, sitting on a bench overlooking the Brooklyn Botanical Gardens' reassuring rose patches, I hauled them out and read:

ADVISOR:

It's difficult to look back on this year and realize how little progress we made with Michael, and how little he himself put into this year . . . He has to learn . . . to find a way to live with structures and rules which he may not like . . . when he walks into class, he becomes more of a performer . . . each of us must realize that (discovering and developing one's identity) has to be done within a framework of order . . . not to the benefit of just one person. Michael has not yet reached this plateau of under-standing, and as a result, his image, unfortunately, is not nearly as good as he likes to think it is. Only a very few of his classmates can honestly relate any genuine admiration for Michael and the way he acts. This is very unfortunate.

SCIENCE:

Michael has virtually done nothing in my class . . . Michael de-cided . . . that science was not his thing . . . The only effort Michael has put into the course is toward disruption of the rest of the class. The year has really been a waste. It is terribly frustrating to watch a capable individual be so obstinate and destructive.

FRENCH:

. . . is not doing as well in French as he could . . . is not keeping up with the work. . . . capable of far better quality work. He still ar-rives in class unprepared at times and his attitude is not very good.

LATIN:

. . . refused to engage himself in the work of the course . . . has much difficulty being a serious, participating member . . . is bright and full of potential, but that potential has yet to be translated into any sort of achievement whatsoever. In a way, it is extraordinary how much Latin he has picked up just from being physically present in the classroom.

RELIGION AND MORALITY:
. . . often expresses sincere interest . . . however . . . attention is turned away from the discussion and his nervous behavior becomes distracting.

This is only a small sample from these report cards; testaments that don't necessarily convey Asperger's syndrome even if they allude to its existence. They instead outline incidents of disrespectful behavior, a lack of effort, failed peer relations, and everyone involved—myself, the teachers, and school officials—as being universally unhappy at the time. As I sat on that bench that day, these reports finally made so much sense (I use them today in certain presentations), and I was even able to feel pity for those teachers for a terrible overall situation that we were *all* in.

While the school years you are reevaluating may seem problematic, for a few of you they may have resonated with real trauma, with experiences far worse than mine, where situations deteriorated to deep levels. The stories I've heard of these instances seem caused not by differing degrees of AS. Instead, they were caused by bad situations that simply deteriorated further than most of us can imagine.

I have oddly enough seen one fairly common characteristic consistently influence the negative school stories of others—a student's inability to maintain eye contact.

I write this chapter having just come off a week of jury duty. In choosing jurors from a pool, one of the questions that was asked of candidates was "How would you determine if someone testifying was lying?" And in almost every instance, potential jurors cited an inability to make eye contact as a key indicator. We have far to go.

Almost every undiagnosed child on the spectrum who shared this characteristic will remember at least one instance of being yelled at with the words, "*Look at me when I'm talking to you.*" Overwhelmed by our own inexplicable inability to do just that, we retreated even further. Without any knowledge of the autism spectrum, an inability to maintain eye contact is inevitably going to be interpreted as deceptive, cowardly, sneaky, and disingenuous. But most of all, it can resonate as a sign of guilt, that whatever the child is being accused of, he did.

Whether in eye contact, or in other forms of nonverbal communication, individuals on the spectrum convey their emotions through means which we have to learn. And since few of us learn to do so to perfection, something will always seem "off" in us. The natural conclusion will be that what we are trying to convey is false. Now here's the confusing part: The *means* with which we are trying to convey such emotions, or thoughts, predominantly *are* false, for they did not come to us seamlessly as they would to others. Our natural choice would probably be to place no emphasis on *how* we convey such thinking at all. But that's not the way the world works, and the mistake that is made herein is that the means with which we communicate may be evident as copied, even fake, yet the emotions conveyed almost never are. This tragic error can easily be blown out of proportion in school situations where AS was not on the list of possible explanations.

Friendships

The possibilities for peer bonding during the school years pose a dilemma for the student with AS:

- We may deeply want to socialize, but don't know how.
- We may deeply want to socialize, yet run from every opportunity.
- When someone is trying to become friends with us, we may miss it completely.
- We may simply not want friends.

During grade school years, I quickly developed an unconscious realization that I was different from my peers. And I compensated by latching on to the most weak-willed kid in my class that I could find, calling him my best friend, and then building a play dynamic around our friendship that was protected, and that no one could enter into and disrupt. For that poor kid, whoever it was at the time, this prevented him from perhaps seeing that something was off in the way I conducted "friendships," as well as prevented him from spending time with kids more like him. But it was at least a way for us to delve deeply into whatever games or toys were of mutual liking. Eventually, the magic would wear off, and he would see that there was a better world out there for him (and I'd have to then go grab someone else). But this tactic completely deteriorated in puberty, when children develop cliques, or friendships in groups, and that was when the real alienation started (as shown on those report cards).

The obstacles put in our way are many. For one thing, since most of us are lacking in fashion sense, we can be ridiculed for what we wear. Hygiene issues having to do with using soap, or brushing one's teeth or hair, may also have played a role. This continues usually until the ridicule gets to be too much, and the individual realizes that he'll have to change (no matter how little sense it may make to the individual) in order to obtain the contact he desires. And then there's the list of typical AS social misfires: entering into conversations too late, failing to restrain what one says (no matter how truthful), inabilities at sports and at seeing what many peers note as appropriate gender behavior—such as submitting to what is typical boy and girl behavior.

Author Donna Williams writes of having abandoned school friendships:

> I was left to roam the streets, which was the most wonderful hands-on discovery learning program a person with autism could have.

For more-challenged individuals, what Williams defends may not work, is not recommended, and may even be quite dangerous. But I shared her experience.

Early in seventh grade I discovered a possible solution to my social deficiencies. During one school day, I and another boy were caught in the bushes on the school campus between classes. He had been smoking a cigarette, and I had merely been talking with him, but the assumption upon our mutual capture was that we were both smoking. We were separated. And the head of the middle school took me into a closed room and asked if I had been smoking. I replied that I hadn't been. He took my fingers and smelled them, and then he asked if the other boy had been smoking. I couldn't lie, but I knew enough about not "ratting out" a peer that all I could do was go silent. He asked repeatedly if the other boy had been smoking, and he was repeatedly answered by my silent, downward gaze. I stayed there alone while he left the room, and when he returned, he told me I should go back to my class, pack up my things, and go home for the day.

When I went back to pick up my schoolbag, my homeroom teacher (normally not a great source for support) was beaming with approval. I didn't understand this at all. Wasn't I supposed to be in trouble? And when I got home, my mother, who'd been called, was radiant with pride. I was stunned.

I'd hit the jackpot. The "noble rebel" mask was the way to go. The iconography of the loner who doesn't care what others think, the outsider with values yet who "runs on the wrong side of the tracks with the wolves," the nonconformist who holds his ethical ground even when under attack . . . this particular brand of exclusion was my means toward inclusion. And I nurtured and utilized this aura well into adulthood with great success (I even learned about the good inside "the wolves"). The joke is that you appear to be someone who doesn't care what others think, when you do care—tremendously so.

Where We May Have Exacerbated the Situation

The subhead above should not be thought of as "blame," or "where we should feel guilty." But there are instances in these difficult pasts where we may have had enough, and in our own way, fought back, making the situation worse but unknowingly doing so for very logical reasons. It helps with the process of these walks to examine them, and actually *removes* such blame.

As my school reports confirm, I became the "class clown" at an early age. Not only had my teachers pushed me so far that I did not concern myself with the sanctity of their classroom, but I also did not understand the difference yet between being laughed at, and being laughed with. My fellow students were incredulous at my relentless behavior, my consistently unfunny jokes, and laughed more as a result—a laughter I mistakenly took to be solidarity. And to further exacerbate the situation, when I realized that my teachers wanted to me to think about myself in negative terms, I consciously refused. I was not willing to let them make me feel less of a person. So I fought back, and in one particular act of defiance (that lasted an entire school year), signed all my papers "Carley the Great."

Such behavior is not unique. Many clinical authors have seen this tendency in undiagnosed kids on the spectrum. As a means of coping with difficult experiences, clinicians cite the child's appropriation of a deity-like persona. And while I personally never felt I was playing ruler of the world, in my case these clinicians are somewhat right. As Dr. Tony Attwood writes in his essay "Diagnosis in Adults," from the book *Coming Out Asperger: Diagnosis, Disclosure, and Self-Confidence*:

> Such children and adults go into "God mode," seeing themselves as omnipotent people who never make mistakes and cannot be wrong . . . Such behaviors may include the use of intimidation and the development of an arrogant and inflexible attitude to achieve authority and control, as others are more likely to "give in" to avoid a confrontation.

But it should be noted that the only alternative to criticisms one doesn't understand is either to fight them or acquiesce to them. Neither choice is pretty, and each has damaging consequences. The damage caused by acquiescing to criticisms you don't understand, agree with, or even see is internal. You take on the opinions of your critics—intimations that you are less of a person, even though you don't understand why—and this internal disliking is very hard to shake off even after you leave school. In fighting the criticisms, however, the individual's consequences are external. More people will be angry at you, and the criticisms escalate to a higher level. But I believe this to be the lesser of two evils. The sense of self held high provides strength, even if the level of esteem one holds oneself at can be unrealistic.

Behavior is the unconscious outlet for confusion in all of us. And in more dramatic cases where the behaviors might have been aggressive, it will help you to understand that this wasn't because you were bad. It was because you, just like everyone around you, were confused. Even the most aggressive, nonverbal autistic person behaves the way he does for a reason. There may be a desire to communicate, there may be internal physical issues that cause panic, as well as pain . . . Many of these reasons have been identified, but many have not.

Other Coping Mechanisms During the Difficult School Years

Many of us on the spectrum have a capacity for being overwhelmed by daydreams. This near-narcotic experience is often described as "retreating into a fantasy world." Whether these are compensatory acts or merely the autistic mind's natural ability is still unknown. But from hearing so many testimonials in GRASP support groups, it appears to be a little of both. The desperate need to focus in on something of interest, coupled with the ability to do so, probably provides children on the spectrum with a means of escaping moments of disinterest or anxiety.

Dr. Temple Grandin writes in her book, *Thinking in Pictures*:

> Autistic fantasies can be confused with hallucinations, but the autistic person knows they are fantasies, whereas the schizophrenic believes they are reality.

Another coping mechanism laced with hard consequences is the ability of an AS child to convince an adult he understands her, even when he doesn't. I did this a lot. When I could not comprehend what an adult was trying to convey, I'd try to trick her. Having realized she did not have the ability to teach me, I tried to nod my head, or say the right things in order to make her go away. I became a great student of what people wanted to hear. My loss was in missing the lesson they were trying to impart, even if I may have saved myself from endless aggravation.

But most of us with AS also have coping skills that were purely beneficial to us during the school years, particularly the independent pursuit of beloved subjects or hobbies. Libraries, record stores, musical instruments, video games, or in fewer cases, even athletic fields can be sources of refuge and safe haven. Being thought of as talented, and therein being given a free pass for many behavioral differences, is a great source of remedy for some undiagnosed children on the spectrum, as it was for me when I was in school. Unfortunately, few kids are lucky enough to have their talents identified.

Conclusion

Great teachers change society for the better, no doubt. But the lousy ones change society too.

While the negative memories will most likely dominate as you look back on your school years, try to find some balancing good memories. We want to see these negatives for what they are, and the examinations can be unavoidably painful. But before School One saved me, I actually had a few moments of great gratitude. In sixth grade, cognitively unaware of what plagiarism was, I went to see a movie, and then wrote an English paper in which I simply copied the plot of the movie I'd just seen. Instead of reprimanding me for what I "should have known," the teacher, Peter Tenney, took me aside and simply instructed me without disappointment as to what was okay and what was not when digesting and becoming influenced by material that has inspired us. I was also treated with some admiration by an English teacher (albeit the stereotypical rebel English teacher who was inevitably fired for drunkenness); and go figure: The varsity football coach—a wonderful man named Jerry Zeoli—saved me from going mad one day when he was the only teacher on the campus who believed me when I truthfully replied that no, I hadn't stolen a car radio out of another teacher's car. I cling as best I can to these three in my recollections of those nine years, and this commitment to remembering them as opposed to the others—others who were simply caught, like me, in the wrong place at the wrong time—serves me well.

Arguably the most effective coping skill is one that is almost always employed after the fact: insight and understanding, knowing why everything transpired the way it did—the knowledge that you will be soaking up perhaps years later. As GRASP member Ruth Snyder writes:

Interpretation of my past was always optimistic but confusing. Now it is less confusing,

As hard as it is, exploring everything that went wrong, and then finding those instances where things could have gone far worse, will help in the process of closure regarding what for almost all of us, whether we are on the spectrum or not, can be very difficult years.

Bullying

Not everyone on the spectrum was bullied, but most were, and what bullying did occur was likely felt more strongly because of the individual's inability to understand why it was happening in the first place. Some grew up with what clinicians now see as small doses of post-traumatic stress syndrome (PTSD) as a result.

The topic of bullying certainly warrants inclusion into any discussion of school difficulties. But bullying extends into neighborhoods, sports teams, family dynamics, and after-school programs, often with greater severity because of the decreased supervision by adults. Furthermore, bullying has become almost a science of its own, and deserves special consideration given all the new thinking provided by Carol Gray's groundbreaking work from a decade ago, and by work that continues today with clinical newcomers like Nick Dubin (himself diagnosed with AS as an adult).

The new thinking has been eye-opening. Gone are the days when we processed such horrors by thinking that the bullies themselves were doomed to unhappy lives. As new studies have shown, bullies don't grow up to become miserable, unsuccessful adults that drink, divorce, and get stuck in dead-end jobs. Contrary to our fantasy of them feeling guilty for their past abuses, they get good jobs, and are often thought of highly in their communities. And it is these former bullies who appear to have perpetuated the self-justifying fallacy that "bullying is just a part of growing up." Their victims, meanwhile, usually struggle as adults. And no victim, unless cursed with a minor-league version of Stockolm syndrome (where you identify and empathize with your tormentors), has likely spoken such self-deprecating words as *bullying is just a part of growing up.*

The recently diagnosed individual will likely want to scan back on these moments, starting with why they were subconsciously identified as targets in the first place. For in addition to all the behavioral differences, children on the spectrum are initially confused by the concept of teasing, and are very prone to being more humiliated by an affront than the neurotypical child generally would be. Many children on the spectrum who displayed motor skill and behavioral differences acted as a homing device for potential predators. Think also of how many of us responded to repetitive teasing by earnestly asking the perpetrators, "Why are you doing that?"—unknowingly making things far worse for ourselves as a result. This communicated to the bullies that they had picked the right target, and only encouraged their antagonistic intent to inflict fear and uncertainty.

GRASP member Gorski recalls:

> I was teased and harassed by so many students for my "differentness." Middle school is brutal in that way; there is no room for eccentricity, and even less room for those who do not know how to be a social networker. I was angry at everyone and miserable.

Others remember similar incidents:

> I was teased constantly. And I didn't understand why my peers weren't accepting me, why they wouldn't let me be their friend . . .
> —Amy Gravino

. . . tormented, beaten up, ostracized . . .

—Michael Lavinger

I would be picked on a lot, called names, "You're ugly," "You're stupid" . . . I didn't get it. I was like, "What am I doing wrong?"

—April Malone

But it is perhaps author Dubin, a GRASP Advisory Board member, who is most remarkable for having suffered many severe instances, and yet who grew up to write about them from a clinical perspective. In his book, *Asperger's Syndrome and Bullying: Strategies and Solutions*, he painfully recalls:

In 1987, I was a third grader at Pembroke Elementary School. One day, a classmate, Stewart, invited me to play with him and another boy, Ralph, after school. I was elated. After all, it wasn't everyday that I got invited to play with someone . . . [Stewart handcuffed] both my arms to the swing and immediately thereafter, he and Ralph took off on their bikes . . . I totally panicked and began shouting for them to come back. The more I screamed, the more I prompted them to taunt me further. The pressure of the handcuffs against my arms was unbearable and the fact that I couldn't move terrified me . . . For about a half hour, I was in an empty park, screaming my head off with no help forthcoming. I was hoping a police officer would drive by and see me. A neighbor. A mailman. Anyone!

Times change. And as more information becomes known about this particular arena of a life lived on the spectrum, more responsibility will be placed on the adults in charge of the environment, not only to provide a safer venue, but also to deal more severely with bullies, whose lax treatment perhaps encouraged them to continue their behavior.

Going further, the behavior of these past tormentors is worth examining. For their predatory instincts can often hold the keys to successful prevention. They are perhaps the ones who first spotted "something wrong" with the individual, not the adults. Heta Pukki, in her essay "Telling Peers at School About Asperger Syndrome: Thoughts on How and Why," in the book *Coming Out Asperger: Diagnosis, Disclosure, and Self-Confidence*, writes:

> Usually, children get to know a peer and define him or her as safe through social play. If they can't find other ways to do this, they will tease the autistic peer until they get a response that they understand, until a description or definition has been produced that makes that child an integrated part of their culture.

I endured only one instance of physical harm from a peer (for the most part, the "wolves" provided me with sufficient protection), when my Boy Scout troop leader punched me in the head during a Scout meeting. However, I had many a frustrated teacher who had given up on reaching me at the elite school I attended before School One. They made jokes directed at me in class (mostly in reference to the suspected drug use), thereby encouraging peer disrespect and laughter. One teacher even called me in, sat me down with one of the brawnier kids in the school, and told me that she was going to instruct the older boy to beat me up if I didn't "clean up my act" (nothing happened).

Teachers, it turns out, are the key ingredient in bullying scenarios that is often missed. As these new books and studies on bullying are released, more and more it is coming to light that teachers often play a very destructive role in abusive situations.

Teachers do not always have control over their students—witness most school classes containing forty-plus students. However, students will often emulate the teacher's attitude. And if the teacher is supportive of a student who is different, then the majority of the students will likely follow suit. But if the child is perceived to be "asking for it," then increased peer isolation will likely be seen by the teacher as somewhat justified. They may even feel, or express, relief and gratitude toward the bullying students.

PAST bullies won't be punished for their past transgressions. The individual walking his walk will be well served to look back with insight, and then move on. Like so much else, and as painful as it is, the bullying of the past will have to be let go.

If real trauma existed, then you will process it more successfully by forgiving *yourself*. Having heard that adage "Bullying is a part of growing up" likely has caused you to blame yourself for still harboring hurt feelings today. Abandon such blame, because bullying is not a part of growing up.

Physical Differences

How can you "spot" a person on the autism spectrum? This varies, for while some may be able to completely mirror neurotypical body movements, others—due to a lack of eye contact, distinctive speech patterns, or a way of merely walking differently—can have identifying characteristics that will set them apart. Looking back on how this played a role is helpful because how others see us affects our lives in many ways. Sexuality, for instance, is prefaced by our capacity for closeness in friendships. And that capacity for friendships will have been influenced by how we physically, as well as behaviorally, appeared at a first glance to others.

Many individuals with AS will have been thought of as clumsy growing up. Because of difficulties in spatial awareness, we have been more prone to bumping into things than our peers, and therein may have acquired a reputation as a "spaz," or worse. This faux-claustrophobia can often lead to awkwardness in navigating just the twisting and turning required to walk through crowded streets. The anxiety this produces, added to the anxiety caused by not knowing why we're filled with anxiety *yet others aren't*—this can cause significant difficulties in travel.

Again, I was often misinterpreted as having "nervous habits." I walked and sat hunched over for most of my childhood, my minor-league version of rocking ruined a few chairs at home, and more surprised than critical, one student during a phys ed class even said to me, "You don't even know how to run." More gravely, though, my eye contact issues were mishandled enough to cause unnecessary eye surgery when I was in fifth grade. (I was blamed for the surgery's lack of success because I "hadn't done [my] eye exercises enough.")

Oddly enough, for many, as it was with me, these issues can improve dramatically. Through sports, yoga, other relaxation techniques—or even peer pressure—we may have willingly or unwillingly compensated by sheer labor.

But for more challenged individuals, or individuals who weren't provided the cognitive awareness of how their movements were perceived, this can pose problems well into adulthood. Airport security checks ("What's up with him?") and encounters with unprepared law enforcement officials can lead to inaccurate conclusions that carry far more damaging consequences.

Speaking Voice

Very often a flat (or monotone) vocal tone sets individuals on the spectrum apart. Be it either a reluctance, an inability, or an initial disinclination, many individuals on the spectrum do not begin their lives knowing when the rest of the world deems it appropriate to shift vocal tone or pitch so as to emphasize—or deemphasize—the text they are saying at a given moment.

And yet seemingly to the contrary, many people also report a childhood talent for copying foreign accents. Liane Holliday Willey, for one, writes about this in her superb book *Pretending to Be Normal*:

> My parents say they were often confused not so much by my ability to copy others, but rather by my desire to do so.

I too shared Willey's ability, to my mother's chagrin. At many an inappropriate moment I would often emulate, say, the clownish German accent learned from watching *Hogan's Heroes*, or the many British accents accrued from watching *Monty Python's Flying Circus*.

Facial Expressions

The person with AS may have also compounded his or her challenges through a difficulty at executing appropriate facial expression. I wasn't that challenged in this area, but I knew I needed improvement. And when the movie *Star Wars* came out in 1977, I noticed that every time Harrison Ford made even the slightest onscreen twitch or wink, the audience exhaled in awe (especially the women). They looked up to him for answers because his facial gestures communicated to them that everything would be all right. He made them swoon, and I wanted that ability too. So I saw the movie fourteen times (granted, I also loved the movie), and after each viewing, I would try out his facial expressions in front of a mirror. Trying them out the first time on live people met with much confusion, if not laughter, from peers. But by the tenth time or so that I tried, I noticed some success.

Sports

While participation in athletics can build character for many children and young adults, it can have the opposite effect with kids on the spectrum. Sports can destroy confidence and increase social isolation in undiagnosed children with AS. Most of the problems lie not only in awkward physical development, but also in the mental concept of being on a team. Unlike failing academically, which doesn't cause other kids to suffer, team sports have a different dynamic: When you fail, you let others down, and this can be a source of further isolation from peers. Statistically dependent games such as baseball certainly have a strong fan base in individuals on the spectrum, but if an interest in *participating* in sports exists at all, it is usually in individual games like tennis or golf. Athletics also require being comfortable with the notion of competition itself, an element that an inadequate-feeling individual may not be able to summon. There are many aspects of our relationship to athletics that bear examining during these walks.

For starters, we usually absorb the rules of sports far later than neurotypical children do. NT kids pick up on the sports-loving nature of their environments quickly, whereas children on the spectrum are busy pursuing their own interests. And later, when games become attractive to us, most children on the spectrum would always prefer to make up rules to their own game rather than do the scholastic work to understand already-existing ones. Sometimes this is merely our sensing that we are behind, and instead of feeling motivated to do the extra catch-up work, the real or imagined exclusionary nature of sports can cause us to quit.

I was actually drawn to team sports partially because of my environment (Providence was a huge sports town), but also because somewhere inside I knew I had so much to learn from the team concept. I played all the larger team sports growing up, and with the exception of baseball, I didn't play them well, nor did I play them for long, nor did I often enjoy my teammates' company. Like others, I suffered from my aforementioned motor clumsiness, I had trouble with balance, and I am supposedly double-jointed in areas. In all sports, my eye issues coupled with existing uncertainty caused frequent misjudgments as to the location of a moving ball. And so somewhere inside, I knew the ball was always a fraction of an inch, or a second in time, from where I thought it was. This caused a lack of confidence that affected my play, even though later, by putting myself in relaxed, hypnotic trances, I often alleviated this. No adult around me knew that these issues were physiological. They interpreted the issues as based entirely on fear, and not knowing any better, I believed this too (though I wouldn't admit it to them).

In baseball—or more specifically, in pitching—I had enjoyed my one athletic gift. I did not have the idolized six-foot-five, 235-pound pitcher's body of the time, nor did I throw a proper overhand. My slender frame throwing sidearm, and at speeds slower than most prospects, I had extraordinary natural movement on whatever I threw. And so by merely throwing at the center of the strike zone, my pitches often found their way to the less-hittable corners of this area. I excelled at the guessing game between hitter and pitcher. And I was a great student of technique, even developing a near-perfect batting swing that unfortunately meant little once the opposing team found out what an awful hitter I was. I wasn't a good all-around baseball player, but baseball was a sport I had a mental knack for. What I was, was a talented pitcher who was lucky enough to be talented at the game I loved the most. Before my changing interests in math, music, writing, theatre, and foreign policy, my first passion was baseball.

One day, when I was nine years old, jealous of kids on TV who got to be batboys of pro teams, I approached the high school baseball coach of my less-than-accommodating school. He took a liking to me and gave me the job. In his eyes, I wasn't a freak, I was someone who loved the game. And so I went to practices and home games, and traveled with the team to road games for three years. This coach was easily my pearl among a sea of destroyed relationships with teachers. From 1974 to 1976, I learned moves and strategies from Coach Jim Maland, and the mental mechanics of the game became to me like a paradise. No clocks—nothing to rush for; the game ended when it ended—and unlike basketball, in which you can just let your best shooter take every shot, in baseball everybody had to wait his turn at the plate, and have his equal moment in the sun.

I played the game in any form I could. With one friend I could play stickball in the winter with tennis balls and sawed-off hockey sticks. And if there were no friends available, I would throw a hard-rubber lacrosse ball (which has a similar weight to a baseball) off a concrete building for sometimes five hours straight. Without knowing, I was ironing out motor skills issues by consistently reacting to the quickness in which the hard-thrown ball came back at me. This activity acted like a hypnotic, highly relaxing trance that made me more accurate and more confident, and which also gave me "chill time" to work out the failures of the day. Nowadays, kids have adventure playgrounds for balance, "hands on hands" teaching for manual dexterity, and in efforts to adjust to fast movements, there are educators trained in slowing the pace of movements, or occupational therapists to iron out issues of lax joints. But before all this advancement, I compensated for my AS through repetitive motion, by repeatedly throwing that hard ball against a concrete wall and catching it, repeating the rhythm over and over again in a physical mantra for hours on end.

Starting when I was twelve, I spent four straight summers at what was regarded as the best baseball camp in the world. Up to then, summer had been the time of my life. The Ted Williams Baseball Camp in Lakeville, Massachusetts, was socially lonely, as the divide between me and my teammates—kids cruelly bent on humiliation, homophobia, and even at times, racism—would keep us eternally separated. But the "jock iconography" that I could not navigate through did not matter on the field. A strike was a strike; and the infuriating prejudices held by my teammates were nullified by our collective desire to win games together. I was so good that they tolerated my long hair, my "retard"-like mannerisms, my seemingly squeamish inability to join in calling others "faggots," and my near-impotence as a hitter at the plate. My ability to pitch was being noticed, and it felt wonderful. A pitcher's mound was developing into a place to breathe, a place of independence and justice, even if it was the justice of revenge, and not closure; the only area where I was remotely looked up to by those who were making my life so miserable. I reveled in the dysfunction, feeling confident, feeling it to be a fun, wonderful circus—the first chaos in my entire life that I could maneuver through with confidence.

It was on these mounds of dirt that I first welcomed being a lightning rod for ire and prejudice. However, the antagonism wasn't based on any misinterpreted behaviors of undiagnosed AS. The jeers I took from the crowd or other teams were again due to my long hair (which had yet to become fashionably accepted). High-strung fathers from all over the country would verbally denounce "that kid" as I swung my head left to right before the first warm-up pitch, intentionally swishing my locks back and forth to rub my differences in the face of an audience of people that I was finally in control of. At the age of twelve, thirteen, or fourteen at these camps, I would frolic in malicious, vengeful glee at hearing from the crowd (usually in a deep Southern accent):

"Boy, if you don't get a hit offa that hippie, you ain't comin' home!!!" (Trust me, I heard this more than once.)

Three offspeed pitches later (to throw a fastball to a tense young man like that would have been a horrible mistake) and the batter slunk back to the bench. And I would allow myself a visible laugh to further needle that father in the stands. I pitied the hitter, but not the hitter's family—not the more culpable adults that fostered such dysfunctionalism. Much of what I loved about my pitching prowess unfortunately involved revenge: hitting back at a world that, outside that mound, always got the better of me. I could willfully display my contempt toward adults without fear of punishment, all because of the circular little hill I was standing on. It was the athletic definition of reprisal—not the scholarly definition, nor the humanist one—and I quietly brought the sports-minded vindictiveness into other areas of my life. This was wrong, and it didn't work. But I so badly wanted to experience, in those other areas, some of the justice, or vengeance, known to me in pitching.

Back home, pitching for my freshman school team in ninth grade, I started every game for a bad team that won only once all year (a win that was close, ending on a pickoff that I made of a runner on second base). The coaches were poor, but I quickly felt the sudden value that was now being placed upon me by the school that was previously unaware of my having any.

But in the last game of the year, with our team up 7–1, I was relieved with two innings remaining. One of the handful of resentful players who'd been begging to pitch all year was put in, and I was taken out. The boy was shelled, and we lost. And as the other pitcher walked off the mound in tears, I overheard the coach tell him something mean. I don't remember what it was, but it was strong enough that, in shock, I looked at the coach, and even though I didn't care all that much for this particular teammate, all I could think of to do to protest such behavior was to grab my glove and throw it down into the dirt as hard as I could.

In my heart, I quit baseball then and there at age fifteen. It was a good move. I knew I was coming up on a decision to choose either pitching or the arts anyway. And unknown to me at the time, I would happily be in a new school the next year, replacing baseball by playing lead guitar in a string of bad high school bands.

Still, what an experience that was . . . Finding peace on a mountaintop is okay, but finding peace when everyone is yelling at you? That made me feel adaptable, that navigating through this strange world was indeed possible.

In actuality, baseball wasn't the only sport I was coordinated at—I could also swim. I was a natural water rat who throughout my childhood refused to leave the water until I was shaking and blue. Alone, underwater, I knew joy. In the small lake beside my grandparents' place in the woods of Northwest Rhode Island, I experienced my only feelings of physical grace. Beneath the surface of the water, I did not feel the nervous and unstoppable snapping action of my arms and legs. With the resistance of the water, my limbs found a fluidity as I tried to catch fish with my bare hands, or played pretend games with myself underwater, games that I never shared with anyone.

I was once asked to compete as a swimmer, and nothing seemed more laughable (laughable as an adult, mysteriously terrifying as a child). To use swimming as a means of revenge, a role that baseball constructively and righteously served me, rang as absurd. Rather than skim the surface swimming faster and faster, I had preferred swimming deeper and deeper, slowly, concentrating on the lungs, and the full extension of my body, performing multiple somersaults and turns in every direction. This was not an arena wherein I wished to spar with others. This was a place of peace.

THE arena of sports is often the one we run the farthest from because of an often-present fear of competition, past traumas, or just an inherent disinterest in everything sports has to offer. But what we risk losing by abdicating the culture of athletics is indeed that comfort with competition—which given the society we live in, could be argued as an outright necessity for success in the neurotypical world. We compete with others for jobs, and more importantly, we compete against *ourselves* in order to improve our lives. As you look back on your years not just in sports, but also in dating and employment, you may find instances where you displayed a reluctance to compete. You were likely looked upon as lacking in effort, or paralyzed by fear to such a degree that it unfairly marred your reputation.

But we don't become gracious winners until we experience winning. And we can't avoid being sore losers unless given the opportunity to experience the pain of losing, even if this is heightened for a significantly affected person on the spectrum. That's what athletics are supposed to give us: a safe arena for emotions that perhaps do not serve us well back in our everyday lives, but that through repeated experience we learn to handle with grace.

Social Life

By now, you will already begin to have a sense as to how the diagnosis affected your social life. I can't imagine anyone on the spectrum whose differences didn't have an impact on his or her ability and desire to create and sustain friendships. Most of you will have had friendships, but perhaps fewer than your peers. Yet many people on the spectrum went through life friendless, were never invited to classmate birthday parties, and never had someone to go out with on a free night. As Adler again writes in "No! You Don't Understand," from the book *Voices on the Spectrum*:

Just because I don't talk to you doesn't mean I don't want to.

Sometimes too individuals on the spectrum will think they have friends, yet don't. The concept of friendship alone being quite vague, some folks with AS may perceive someone who just says hello in the hallway as a friend. Starved for companionship, many will even call bullies their friends when referring to them with others or family members.

Getting to know author Stephen Shore has taught me a lot about my own history of friendships, and relationships in general. Stephen, who is married to a Chinese woman, talks often about how it sometimes can be easier relating to someone from another culture. If they themselves feel out of sync with the society they find themselves in, it often helps them to draw closer to someone else who also seems slightly out of sync. When I worked for the veterans organization, I noticed that many Vietnam veterans had significant others who were either of another culture, or who were significantly older or younger than they. This made sense in that there was such a feeling of disconnectedness with the society they'd returned home to after the war. However, unaware of my diagnosis when I worked for them, I never made the connection regarding myself. I should have, though: Almost every girlfriend I had in college was from another country, but at the time I attributed the reasons to the self-promotional notion that I was perhaps more cultured than my peers.

There have always been people who have enjoyed my company, but more than the usual share of people who didn't. This got better in time once I made the effort to listen for my fair percentage of any conversation (i.e., talk for 50 percent of the time in a two-person conversation, 33 percent for a three-way, 10 percent if the other person needs to get something off his chest, and so on) and it also got better once I figured out when it was okay to stray from the topic, and when it wasn't. But this was hard. Sometimes a conversation that doesn't interest you isn't just boring, it's agonizing, and it puts you at great risk for offending your conversation partner.

I have also never kept in touch with old friends the way most people do. I never saw the need. Outside whatever profession I've been in, I have enjoyed, and needed, very few "friends." But I have always needed to have a very strong bond with people that I work with. I connect with them over a sense of shared purpose, and I *choose* to be content with this version of camaraderie because it fulfills me immensely.

As you walk your walk, you may recall plenty of incidents where people were indeed trying to reach out to you, where you simply did not see the extension of companionship as it was being offered. But there's also the possibility you may have seen it yet rejected it, or inadvertently communicated rejection.

There is also the delicate subject of maturity. Individuals on the spectrum are often seen in a positive light as having a child-like exuberance and enthusiasm; the word *pure* is sometimes used. That's the "glass half-full" side. But those wishing to see us in a negative light will throw the word *immature* in our direction. Owing to peer differences, we are often shut out of developmentally appropriate experiences. In such cases, no, we will not emotionally grow alongside our peers, even if we invest our energies elsewhere, and grow in different ways as a result.

And while our natural instinct for taking things literally will affect *all* the areas covered in this chapter, our tendency toward literalness is perhaps most influential on our capacity to make friends. It was one thing as a child for me to hear, "Let's toast the bride and groom," and recoil in horror, because looking back, this is pretty funny. But when GRASP facilitator Cathy Collins was taking graduate classes after college, she had a more debilitating experience when her sister was diagnosed with terminal cancer:

> I had told a teacher at graduate school about her illness. I considered the teacher to be a role model and was, therefore, more than ready to believe that she was seriously interested in my well-being. She told me to call her if I needed to talk. When my sister died, I really needed someone to talk to, so I called her. As I recall, she seemed surprised and perfunctory on the phone. She said she was sorry, but did not ask me to come in to talk with her face-to-face and did not talk over five or ten minutes on the phone.

I hung up feeling more isolated and lonely than ever—also feeling that I had made a fool of myself.

What's a Friend?

The level or number of friendships we have had in our lives hopefully wasn't what it was because of any scripts that we were supposed to adhere to. Hopefully it was based on desire, or need. Writing this reminds me that there *are* some friends that I have stayed close to for many years—my friends Les, Ron, and Steven. These three are all significantly successful photojournalists I've known since the 1980s, and the common question I used to ask myself was, "Considering what I now do for a living, what draws me to these three as friends?" We've always played cards together, we've enjoyed behaving relatively infantile with one another, and we genuinely like each other. But that aforementioned purpose of work-related friendships doesn't apply to them anymore. So why are we still together?

Ron may have logged more time covering the Bosnia war and its atrocities than anyone else; Steven lives most of the year in Colombia; and Les has covered wars all over. Having seen, from my limited time in Bosnia and other places, examples of human behavior that are out of the norm, it comforts me to have friends that don't find such experiences to be uncomfortable or intimidating to talk about. And though I got shot at only twice, they know that they are with someone who appreciates and shows consideration for the severity of their work, as they experienced whatever I did a thousand times more. We rarely talk about this stuff (we see each other maybe only twice a year). But they understand how those experiences helped shape me, and I, in turn, am someone outside their profession who respects all that they have accomplished and sacrificed.

Not the normal script for friendship, no. But big deal. There's desire, need, gratitude, and a strange commitment to continuance with every year that passes.

Alcohol and Drugs

I drank. Born into an Irish-Catholic paternal side, I started drinking at an early age because it was socially acceptable to do so. But I also drank because it was a means of connecting with potential friends, even with family members that I loved. Back then, there was a culture surrounding alcohol. And in later years, I embraced the iconography of the fun, drunk playwright because of society's erroneously positive look on such things—an interpretation that for the greater good has thankfully begun to disappear.

But as a child I'd watched many relatives enduring alcoholism-related failures in relationships, jobs, and health; and having seen what they'd gone through, I carried with me the knowledge that someday I would have to quit. This came true in 1991 when I was twenty-seven years old, a little over a year into my first marriage. The "quit now" indicator was that I suddenly wasn't a happy drunk anymore. I hadn't lost a job, nor was my marriage threatened at the time, but over my last three months of drinking I had become a destructive and sour drunk.

Having quit at an early stage of alcoholism, I've heard both yes and no viewpoints as to whether I fit the description of an alcoholic. While I had little trouble quitting, and never needed Alcoholics Anonymous or any such equivalent, I was feeling healthier than I'd ever known was possible after two years of being "dry." But just for a moment, let's say that I am an alcoholic (as a therapist at the time assured me I was). If this is true, then I carry the dreaded burden of being a recovering alcoholic who is eternally grateful that I drank. Due to the era, and the culture, and the social constraints that I grew up under, I would have had little if any social life outside my teenage musicianship had I not drunk. Do I then want to encourage young individuals on the spectrum to drink? Absolutely not. The world has gotten infinitely smarter about choosing its role models. But the world can get even better at making the social playing field fairer and more behaviorally permissive so that kids don't have to risk rolling the dice with their futures in order to have friends.

The concept of drinking in moderation can often seem very sound to the individual on the spectrum, and most will drink responsibly. Also, as society's messages about the pitfalls of overuse become clearer, we understand them more. *When* you grew up will probably have played a pivotal role in how you view or use alcohol because society's attitudes about it are ever-changing.

That said, there's obviously a big difference between alcohol and illegal substances: One's legal. The other is not. This will, and should, play a role in our decision-making process when we're about to purchase something or put it inside our bodies.

Compared to the rest of the population, few individuals on the spectrum seem to gravitate toward illegal substances. It just doesn't seem to pragmatically compute whatsoever. But those who do engage in such risky behavior seem to do so strictly as a means toward social contact—to fit in rather than lash out. Substance abuse tends to seem pointless to most of us, owing to our sensibilities, our fears, or our need for control.

That said, this is a largely unexplored phenomenon. Substance abuse might very well *disguise existing spectrum conditions*, possibly preventing them from being noticed and subsequently identified. If true, this would mean that even more adults than we're aware of are awaiting proper diagnosis and treatment.

Dating

Out of all the topics discussed in GRASP support groups, the two that participants demand be repeated every year are employment issues and dating—and by the latter I mean *getting* a date as well as succeeding once you're on one. While many individuals on the spectrum are struggling to obtain jobs and significant others, many are also working hard to *hold on* to jobs and significant others.

Failed dates are another source of embarrassing memories. Our impaired ability to distinguish between those who have an interest in us, and those who don't, is a challenge. I too was lousy at this guesswork unless the person made it painfully obvious. I needed brazen proclamations of attraction, or the opposite, disdain (wherein the person wanted nothing to do with me), in order to correctly gauge someone's interest in me. Only if given a clear sign would I ask someone out.

I surely missed many opportunities when others were trying to communicate interest in me. When I was in between my two marriages, I couldn't recognize suggestive looks without the inhibition-killing alcohol of my earlier years. And what I needed people to say to me—and I do mean "say"—was, "I'd like to get to know you better," "I'd like to go out on a date with you," or whatever the case may have been. Because the rest of the world doesn't usually operate literally (which to them can feel like a contract negotiation, thereby taking a lot of the fun out of the chase), needless to say, I was plagued by feelings of stupidity for blown chances.

By now, the reader should have enough of a keen sense of all the nonverbal communication challenges that seamlessly translate into the arena of dating—I won't rehash. But what deserves some extra consideration is perhaps the anticipated ritual of what a "date" is supposed to mean. Usually there's asking someone out, arranging the date (usually dinner and something akin to a movie), a ton of small talk over a meal, and then the ambivalence of whether the timing is right or not for any level of intimacy or physical contact. I haven't made that sound attractive because, from all I've heard and experienced, such rituals usually aren't.

Before my first marriage, I was lucky. I never had to date in this manner. Again, there was alcohol, which quelled many inhibitions; but more important, I had enough positive iconography surrounding my abilities that I was considered attractive enough to get by without engaging in the scripts of traditional dates. But after my divorce, when I was a nondrinker in my thirties, women expected the traditional date. Were my "between marriage" dinner dates disastrous? No, but there was enough discomfort suffered by both parties that the date usually ended in a handshake with no plans for another. As I'll discuss further looking back on our histories relating to sexuality, I learned early on that my best chance at someone being attracted to me was in being seen passionately involved in whatever work or task I was engaged in. From there, the ability to avoid the ritualistic "date" was much easier.

Because we are different from the rest of the world, often it takes, not concessions, but a different mind-set in our potential significant others to be able to see past our differences and find qualities they like. Holliday Willey again provides another beautiful example in *Pretending to Be Normal* as she recalls someone she once knew:

> To him I was a friend he liked to do things with, someone to share life with for a while. He never batted an eye when he saw I lived with two dogs and five cats, instead of a bunch of girls. He never expressed any concern over my weird habit of grilling people for way too much information. He always stood by me patiently when I freaked out from having had too much sensory stimulation. He never questioned me or criticized me, he just let me be. If only everyone could be that gracious—maybe then, we would not even need a definition of Asperger's Syndrome.

However, as we smugly denounce conventional dating traditions, it must be held that others may very much need the routine of the dinner/movie date, or that the signals at the end of the date (for physical contact, for whether a second date is desired, etc.) be interpreted correctly. And it is not fair for us to judge that need. Such convention may not be the best solution for individuals on the autism spectrum, but that does not make it universally wrong by any means. As you look back on your dating history, you will be well served to accept that perhaps certain relationships were not meant to be. This is hard, because most of us desire intimacy, and we will have endured more than our fair share of rejection. That rejection, if built up over time, risks making us so embittered that we squash further attempts at such happiness right from the start. We'll be too scared. And we'll give in to impulses of fear that we might interpret as self-preservation.

In order for that not to happen, the rejection must be released— learned from, laughed at perhaps, and then let go. Furthermore, there are other roads to take toward more successful dates that we may not have taken before—roads to be discussed in Chapter 5.

Sex

Learning to discuss sex openly should not be intended to fulfill anyone's political aims, or to go against the religious and moral principals of any particular individual. It's simply important to discuss *any* difficult issue in life because it decreases the anxiety that will only compound already existing problems. Anything that is important to us in our lives carries a cost: It can breed more than the usual share of stress when all does not go as planned.

While there will be many of you who are satisfied with your sexual past, present, and future, there will be many for whom the subject has been a source of frustration. Many of the reasons for dissatisfaction are reflected in the same dilemmas embedded in socialization and dating. After all, even individuals who aren't on the spectrum often have conflicted feelings about sex, particularly when they look back on their first sexual experiences. Add the confusion of AS (and even more so, undiagnosed AS), and you've got a recipe for complicated, uncomfortable feelings.

Problems

Most of us—either in school, at home, or on the streets—receive sex education of some kind, albeit to varying degrees of usefulness. Some schools have sexual education courses (with varying degrees of quality), and some do not. Some of us come from families that were comfortable discussing sex with us, and some—perhaps for understandable cultural or religious reasons—were not comfortable at all. Some of us had the social skills to gain dubious knowledge from peers, and some of us did not have this option. There will be fewer problems for those of you who had sex ed, parents comfortable with the subject, and developmentally typical peer relations. And there will be greater confusion and anxiety for those of you who may have had a combination of the opposite.

There are indeed sexuality curriculums for kids who need it. Yet even some of the best existing curriculums have remarkable inconsistencies. In his sexuality talks, Dr. Peter Gerhardt, the President of the Organization for Autism Research, cites a court case he testified in about a young man with a challenging degree of AS. The young man was arrested after repeatedly going to a certain mall where he approached women and asked them, "May I touch your breasts?," "May I touch your vagina?," and so on. No small wonder he was arrested. However, upon examination, this young man was simply doing what he was told by his sexuality instructors, who had merely conveyed the common instruction that when he wanted to touch someone, he had to ask.

Also, some of us would like to have a lot of sex in our lives, others would prefer a more moderate amount, and a few others want little or none. And you may have therefore felt estranged from greater society, if not potential partners, no matter what your preferences are. Media outlets, for instance, such as film and television (not to mention the pornography world) can leave you feeling that if you don't want a ton of sex in your life, then there's something very wrong with you. Yet on the other end, prevailing curriculums and sexuality trainers tend to do the same damage in the opposite direction. For clinical attitudes currently have a distinct preference for the "less sex" side of this paradigm, greatly favoring the idea that more atmospheric sex, and more spiritually connected sex, is the only way to go. In the long-term sense over a person's sexual lifetime, it probably is indeed the most fulfilling. But this isn't right for everyone, nor is it realistic to expect it to happen during every sexual encounter, and until these curriculums learn to be more inclusive of sexual pluralism, they will continue to make certain individuals feel like terribly insensitive sexual partners. This does just as much damage as the media messages that suggest you're a terrible sexual partner if you desire sex less.

If you have indeed been made to feel as though you are less of a person for what you desire out of life, try not to give it much thought. For such an emphasis on atmosphere and karmic connection (usually spotted by an overusage of the word *intimacy*) is highly unrealistic to expect in every sexual encounter. And on the flip side, everyone else is *not* having great sex six times a day. Preferences about sexual frequency should be made out to be just as natural as anyone else's.

Pornography is particularly important to discuss as it is turned to by many people who do not enjoy fulfilling sex lives, especially men. This carries highly politicized and highly debatable pros and cons. The most obvious pro is that it keeps the desire for sexual contact alive during times when we are experiencing repeated failures at connecting with other people. The con is that it can give a highly unrealistic portrait of what a normal sex life looks like. Pornography, by design (ask any industry person), is about fantasy. Certainly we can expect sexual partners to cater to fantasies every once in a while, but when an individual repeatedly views porn, many problems can surface:

- The viewer decides that fulfilled fantasies are the only way to enjoy sexual contact.

- The viewer expects to be as physically desired as the porn actors pretend to be on film; therefore, they can get mad if the partner doesn't always find them "so hot" as is exaggerated in porn through fake moans and sexual aggressiveness.

- The viewer concludes bitterly that the rest of the world is having a great time while he is not.

- The viewer becomes convinced that if someone doesn't have a body similar to that of a porn star, then they aren't attractive.

Such unrealistic expectations may have set you up for a great deal of disappointment once you obtained, or attempted to obtain, a sexual relationship.

And while frustrated and challenged males on the spectrum may often turn to porn, frustrated and challenged women on the spectrum, especially younger ones, can often fixate on celebrities. The fixations, rooted more in seeking a connection rather than in the physical desire to have sex with them, often leave them convinced that they would be a good match for this distant object of their affection. The unrealistic obtainability of such a relationship seems to work as somewhat of a ruse to hide (especially from themselves) that the individual might be giving up on the idea of ever enjoying a genuine relationship.

Others are better able to mirror the rest of the world, have sexual experience, and don't suffer the same level of sexual anxiety as their more-challenged peers on the spectrum. But there can still be challenges. Heterosexual women may have sensed that one avenue they have for connecting with another person is sex. And they may have used this road strategically more than

Many experts cite how few cases there are of people on the spectrum committing sexual assault, especially when compared with their capacity to be the victims of such violence.

was wise. Without proper knowledge of the dangers of using their bodies in such a way, many women fall victim to an unwanted reputation (yes, even in this day and age), and can become at frighteningly high risk for sexual assault or unwanted pregnancy, and both genders risk sexually transmitted diseases.

Oddly enough, nonheterosexual relationships seem to be less charged with the potential for trauma. Certainly there are still prejudices to navigate through in gay and lesbian relationships, but people of similar gender already have somewhat of a bond—gender differences are one less hurdle to jump over. Theory-of-mind issues—believing that the other person is thinking the same thing as you—seem less consequential in same-sex relationships. And at the risk of angering some of my gay and lesbian friends, I would have to confess to having seen what I believe are naturally heterosexual people on the spectrum who enter gay and lesbian relationships and thrive in them. But the goal for all of us is usually love. And when love is offered where no love seemed possible before, I personally hope that the individual takes such an opportunity. For to dissuade someone from reciprocated love, based on someone else's possible objections and biases, could deny them what has to be the greatest experience the human race is capable of.

Sensory issues play a huge role in our sexual history as well. Most individuals on the spectrum enjoy deep-tissue contact (big hugs) more than the next person, and so they can't wait to get to the more passionate portion of an encounter. And yet you might have experienced difficulty with the light touch, which is often an ingredient in the world's standard idea of how foreplay should be enacted. Some of you may even detest this light touch so much that it has prevented you from being able to *get to* the deep-tissue contact that you might enjoy (i.e., the actual sex), because you don't want to engage in that foreplay. Lighting, sounds—perfumes and colognes too—all kinds of environmental factors may influence the possible encounter in a way that can make bedroom success seem implausible. And the anxiety caused by such obstacles can also affect the libido.

The sensory world's impact on sexuality goes far deeper than I'll describe herein. But to give just one example: Isabelle Hénault, in her book *Asperger's Syndrome and Sexuality*, states that in some cases:

> Tactile hypersensitivity can cause vaginal penetration to be pain-
> ful for some women with AS.

Anxiety may have sadly dominated many of your attempts at a healthy sex life—a problem also seen in neurotypical individuals. Whether it's worrying about performance or attractiveness, or being able to pick up the signals that someone is attracted to us—this is challenging. Furthermore, the sense of social disconnectedness, and (as stated in Chapter 1) the often unreported sexual traumas that may have occurred, can all play a role in an individual simply giving up on a healthy sex life. My hope is that those of you who have experienced this can give it another try; this time armed with better information. I would certainly understand if you cannot at the moment. But perhaps someday . . .

Why Do These Problems Exist?

As stated earlier, the majority of the world gathers information about sex from peers, usually long before sexual contact is obtained, if it ever is. And if you were denied certain peer experiences, you may have missed out on simple, generalized lessons about what the sexual act entails (which usually starts out with just as much inaccurate as accurate information). We also need our families to play a role in our sexual education if we expect our sexual lives to reflect a typical society. But some families are not equipped to take on this role.

The next developmental step is experience; and if we experience comparatively less than our peers, we'll probably figure that out, and feel bad about it in the comparative grand scheme of things. Experience counts, because experiences not influenced by trauma are what lead to confidence.

Other problem issues with those of us who are more-challenged have to do with:

- Recognizing that the neurotypical world is not a place where it is automatically okay to talk about sex (we need to talk, but we have to pick our spots as to where and when).

- Understanding the meaning of the word *stalking* so that it can be avoided. Even though this is not a sexual issue, it is worth noting that those of us who fixate on someone usually cannot see (or are too afraid to see) the signals that our feelings aren't reciprocated. By continuing to pursue someone, the individual almost always means no harm. But the rest of the world does not know this. And there are plenty of stalkers who do mean harm, so that the neurotypical world's condemnation of stalking in general is extremely justified.

- Consciously recognizing when someone is touching himself or herself in public. Masturbation of any kind is done because it feels good, and doing it in private is never wrong. But because it feels so good, more-challenged individuals find it hard to understand why they can't do it anywhere. Obviously, people can get in a great deal of trouble herein as well because it is against the law to become nude, or to perform *any* sex act, including masturbation, while in public. Often, this problem is due to the fact that . . .

- Many more-challenged individuals on the spectrum are denied sex education because those in charge of their care feel that their condition negates the need for such instruction. This is horribly wrong, and not just because a life of shared intimacy might be possible. While our wiring may be different, the development of our bodies usually mirrors that of everybody else. And the changes that occur in puberty scare all of us if we don't know what's happening.

For less-challenged individuals who are in the midst of relationships, there may be problems similar to what the rest of the world experiences, such as unappealing routines that are hard to break out of, or one or more parties starting to lose interest. Again, the rest of the world goes through this too, but where we may need to take note is that it may have been harder for us to resolve the issues. What probably helped, however, is that most of us have a distinctly loyal demeanor, in that when problems arose, you probably didn't look elsewhere (i.e., to cheat), and instead stuck it out with your partner longer than the next person would.*

---

*Before we tip our cap to ourselves too much regarding loyalty, however, remember too that the idea of cheating, or moving on to a new relationship, is usually more intimidating to us than it is to others. We like our routines too much to try to juggle "sneaking around," which is usually a very risky, very uncertain form of behavior.

For my part, I long ago learned that the rest of the world did not appreciate it when I would openly discuss sexual matters. I cognitively understand now that if I want to succeed, I cannot often do this. But I *instinctively* haven't changed. I still privately wonder why we all can't discuss the subject as freely as we might a baseball game. It may be illogical to me, but what I had to learn was that being logical wasn't the point. My ideal of what the terrain of life should look like doesn't often compare to what the terrain actually looks like.

But for those of you who have not been so lucky or able, frustration with a lack of sexual experience can be an enormously polarizing experience. And owing to the social constraints thrust on spectrum individuals, many of us have had this difficulty. Like all else, cognitively understanding your diagnosis will do much to repair the social banana peels that emerge when you try to get to know someone on a level deeper than friendship.

Job History

As with dating, we can divide this subject into "obtaining" and "maintaining." For individuals trying to find employment, picking an appropriate job to pursue, creating a résumé, and succeeding in the interview process can be a daunting experience.

Without knowing you had AS, some of you may have displayed behavioral characteristics of the diagnosis during past interviews: You may have shown physical tics, a monotone manner of speaking, a difficulty with reciprocal conversation, or difficulties with eye contact—any of which may have scared off the interviewer. Some individuals who are more affected may also have had difficulties with realistic assessments of what abilities they have and do not have at a given point in their lives. No matter where we lie on the spectrum, we get ideas about how the world works, especially regarding employment fields, and these ideas are usually embedded in our psyches because the ideas seem to be incredibly logical assessments. Because of this, we assume these ideas to be true depictions of how the world works. I just recently spent a long time trying to convince a challenged and unemployed young man that:

1. It isn't a good thing to wait around until a car hits you so you can collect a big legal settlement, and

2. Getting hit by a car and collecting a big settlement probably won't happen (his response every time I intimated this was, "But it *could* happen, right?").

The long and short of it is that probably everyone on the spectrum has endured some job problems caused by his or her diagnosis, but most of the time they're caused by the social interaction required of each job rather than the actual work we do. Anxiety, social demands, and sensory issues can contribute to our feeling overwhelmed when we're supposed to be enjoying that great capacity to bury ourselves in our work. For the most part, every employment field has social rules and varying degrees of behavioral permissibility that have to be understood.

Let's think of another spectrum: a spectrum of work fields.

Spectrum of Behavioral Permissibility in the Workplace

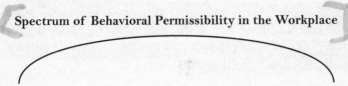

Now if we were to think of what work field allows the greatest diversity in physical, vocal, or cerebral gestures, we would probably come up with . . .

Spectrum of Behavioral Permissibility in the Workplace

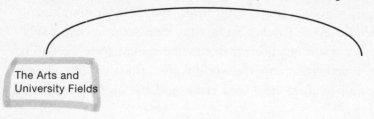

Professors, writers, musicians . . . So long as you're good at what you do, you probably will get a free pass for your "oddness."

So what goes on the opposite end, the reverse extreme wherein no behavioral permissibility seems to exist?

Spectrum of Behavioral Permissibility in the Workplace

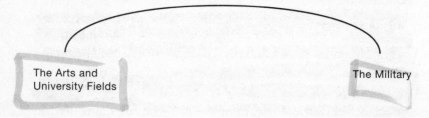

Obviously, it's the military. *But* . . . here's the weird twist: The military could be seen as being just as attractive to individuals on the spectrum as the arts. In the military, they pretty much tell you exactly what to do from the moment you wake up until the moment the lights are turned out. Whom you can address, how to address them, what happens during the entirety of your day. In the military, as compared to other fields, you have things to do, and you certainly have tension, but there is significantly less that you have to socially interpret yourself.

Spectrum of Behavioral Permissibility in the Workplace

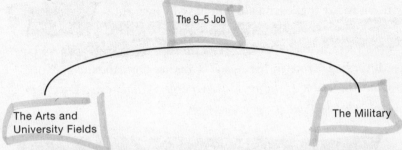

The 9–5 Job

The Arts and
University Fields

The Military

It's the middle ground, the nine-to-five office job, where we slip on the most banana peels. Because in these environments the social rules are always the most complicated, they're never explained, and they're different in each office. Furthermore, turnaround is vast and frequent in these fields, which leads to a feeling of expendability and replicable value on every worker (in other words, tons of people could probably do this job). And when this happens, greater emphasis is put on how the worker socially fits in with colleagues as well as on *how* the job gets done, rather than just the job getting done. Unfortunately, the nine-to-five office environment is the work field where most people end up.

Scattered elsewhere on this spectrum are:

- Technical and mechanical fields, which can be soothing to work in, as well as being paradoxically confusing environments to work in.

- Manual labor, which doesn't put stresses on the mind like other jobs, but such work relies solely on your body, and our bodies have limitations if they become overworked.

- Self-employment, which provides great flexibility with hours and socialization demands, but which still requires enormous networking, and is a work area that few with AS succeed at.

Without going over every possible arena of employment, suffice it to say that each field will have its own rules. Even IT fields, wherein we think of people sitting in a basement somewhere . . . even these fields have their level of required socializing. As Jane Meyerding wrote in her essay "Coming Out Autistic at Work," from the book *Coming Out Asperger*: *Diagnosis, Disclosure, and Self-Confidence*:

> Given how much interaction is required by most jobs, it can feel as if we are working two jobs simultaneously.

In my past playwriting career (endured for eleven years before I'd ever even heard the word *Asperger's*), I was abominable at selling myself. I got produced, I never got bad reviews, and my working relationships were often quite wonderful. But selling oneself is a skill we all need in order to succeed in the work world, regardless of our career choice. Small wonder that I was lousy at this—in thinking I was just like everyone else, I adhered to the "just be yourself" strategy, which no doubt put people off. And so I was broke, thanks to my inability to network myself into more successful circles and larger productions. But at the time, not knowing about my AS, how could I sell myself when I didn't have a clue as to what I was trying to sell?

When I was in college, one of my theatre professors consistently went out of her way to get me in contact with successful alumni who worked in the field. I blew all these chances, though I was so oblivious to the failures that the memories resonate with far more comedy than they do tragedy. Once she secured a phone interview between me and the documentary filmmaker Ken Burns. Burns, coming off the success of his Civil War documentary, was about to hit megastardom through his documentary on baseball. He was extremely cordial to me on the phone. And after asking what I had done and studied, he asked if I had any interest in film, indicating that he might find work for me if that were the case. Now, most of the time, if you did theatre, you were supposed to take film jobs as they could lead to contacts to help your theatre career. I didn't know this, so I blankly told him no. Taken aback, he very politely told me that he only wanted people who had an interest in film (after all, he worked in film). Surprised, I said, "Oh . . . okay," and I then thanked him for his time and walked away from the phone thinking that I had done a masterful job because I'd had such a polite conversation with such a famous person.

When I first got out of a graduate school, I was armed with my prestigious master's degree in playwriting, a piece of paper whose immediate economic potential might have found better use slipped under the bottom of a birdcage. So, I bounced from one "stupid day job" to another, almost entirely in offices, in an attempt to consistently pay my rent. At each job, I would make a good first impression: Employers liked that I would quickly assess what my responsibilities were, and I always tried to work harder than anyone else around me. But I did two things consistently wrong.

Not knowing when it was, and when it was not, okay to take a break and socialize, I just never took such breaks. I'd instead bring work from other jobs to do during downtime. This was inevitably taken to mean I did not like my coworkers. I usually had little in common with them, true, but I did not dislike them. Also, after assessing what my work responsibilities were, my mind would go further, and I would quickly get an idea of how the whole place should be run. Unfortunately, my assessment of how the business should run did not reflect the boss's. And I could not, for the life of me, understand how his version could possibly differ from mine. Was my idea better than his? Well, actually, no, because there were so many variables of the needs of the business that I was unaware of. But based on what I knew, my idea just had such a convincing logic to it.

Now, let's say my way was better—it never was, but just for the sake of argument let's pretend . . . The real truth here is that it doesn't matter whose way is better. The boss's way of doing things is what you *have* to learn because he's the boss and you're not (yet). If the boss doesn't think you're doing what he wants you to do, you probably won't work there long. It's as simple as that. If bosses want your ideas on how the business should be run, they'll ask. But just remember, they usually don't ask. The young man who couldn't be convinced out of waiting for a car to hit him so he could collect on a large insurance claim? That impulse, that same gathering of assessments of how the world works, and finding so much logic to it that you can't see otherwise—that was quite simply a more exaggerated version of what I went through.

GRASP member Jeffrey H. Baer has been through several jobs due to many of the aforementioned social challenges:

> I simply think they lost out on a top-notch employee who could do the jobs well if they bothered to give me a real chance.

MANY people on the spectrum identify with characters from previous and present versions of the television show *Star Trek.* "Data" is the character many younger people identify with, yet having never seen the newer version of the show, I can't comment. But I definitely remember the character of Mr. Spock, from the first incarnation of the show. And while many people will identify with Spock's logical way of thinking, we admired him not for his cerebral prowess. We admired him more because it never bothered him that his way of doing things was so different from everybody else's. In his own way, Spock had a thick skin that we all desired.

Yet we also *envied* Spock, for he enjoyed a workplace environment that (albeit, sometimes condescendingly) appreciated his gifts. There were many episodes where his unique problem-solving strategies were recognized by his peers as the right course of action despite their inability to have thought of such strategies themselves. Spock wasn't second in command for nothing. And that we still envy this—some forty years after these episodes aired—shows how far we still have to go.

More Dramatic Consequences

Like others who seek to be what they are not, we invariably end up with secondary problems engendered by chronic anxiety. As rage and frustration are pushed below our consciousness, we suffer depression. Somatic difficulties like stomachaches and headaches and other ailments can be chronic as a result of unrelenting anxiety and the repression of coping mechanisms while trying to fit in. Painful memories of past failures to be normal and mounting evidence of our inadequacies, our failed attempts to "fit in" dog us.

—Dawn Prince-Hughes, Ph.D., *Songs of the Gorilla Nation*

I often get jealous when speaking with people who work with children on the spectrum. They are dealing with what can only be thought of as a very "pure" autism or AS, wherein all the signs are more easily shown, and hopefully accommodated. Because every once in a while I will see someone in a GRASP support group whose early misdiagnosis led to misprescribed pharmaceuticals, which had damaging side effects, which led to further misdiagnosis, which led to further misprescribed pharmaceuticals, and so on and so on. And the end result is an individual for whom I have to dig through layer upon layer of justifiable anger and trauma just to touch the diagnosis that is so much more easily seen in a child.

These are the exceptions, not the norms, but there are enough of these hard-luck stories to warrant inclusion herein, especially in the desire to broaden your scope of just how far all this new information really extends. Think of all the people who were permanently institutionalized in, say, the fifties and sixties, perhaps misdiagnosed with far more severe conditions, still sitting there, perhaps near-comatose—how many of them could have been properly diagnosed today, and accommodated? How many undiagnosed individuals are languishing in jail who, if properly identified, might have traveled down less-desperate paths?

For starters, children who were misdiagnosed with more severe conditions may have found themselves in highly inappropriate school placements. As Clare Sainsbury writes in *Martian in the Playground*:

> Mixing children together with a great variety of special needs could also expose children with Asperger's to possible manipulation and victimization by emotionally and behaviorally disturbed children.

GRASP member Gregory H. Gorski agrees:

> I was also sent to a lousy Special Ed school for two years that ruined my high school years, as I never learned anything that was actually required by a real high school while going there. I also

became severely disenchanted with the Special Ed mindset of never allowing anything actually negative to be said. Special Ed's ultra-PC mindset of never allowing anything actually critical to be said did not work with my Aspergian tendency to call things as they actually appear to be without sugar-coating it.

Most of these educational situations employ strategies that have little chance at success for students with AS even if the student has been properly diagnosed. Sainsbury again provides great clarity in writing that:

> Behavioral approaches which rely on rewards and punishments can only work to motivate someone to do what they are capable of doing; they cannot provide someone with the cognitive tools necessary to be able to control their behavior at times of stress.

The dramatic upshot herein is that depending on the severity of the behavior, the time you lived in, or the frustration level of the people around you, the behaviors exhibited may have had far worse consequences than mere stigmatization. Not everyone has the patience, competence, or experience to address severe behaviors by looking for medical pain, sensory pain, unexpressed severe anxiety, or the causes behind the frustration that leads to the behaviors.

Louise Flying Thundercloud is a GRASP member and a Cherokee Blackfoot and Maroon Indian. She has been through the wringer as a "troublemaker" who exhibited behaviors that required a real expert to correctly diagnose. She got her diagnosis, but late:

> I had been diagnosed as being paranoid schizophrenic, bi-polar & given all types of medicine . . . I had dreaded behavior issues. I

was in physical fights most of my 20's & 30's . . . I wanted to be as far away from people most times . . . In December of 2005, when the doctor said, "by the way, you have Aspergers Syndrome & that is a form of autism", I felt bells going off in my head. I was thinking to myself, oh so that is why you don't like people very much, that is why you don't like to have close friends, that is why you were in so many fights, that is why people wanted to beat you up because you could not stop picking at people or telling jokes that were not funny at all, that is why you get in trouble on jobs because you don't know the difference between who likes you & who does not.

This subsection opens many a can of worms, and admittedly does not do the topic justice. The few readers who will have shared such experiences should take heart: Gorski now attends an honors program at a distinguished university, and Flying Thundercloud is bravely discovering what she can do in her life, as opposed to what she can't do, while dealing with a significantly more challenged autistic daughter.

But for the majority of recently diagnosed folks, it is helpful, and hopefully not scary, to ponder the massive implications that your diagnosis presents—not necessarily to acknowledge this awful part of the past, but rather to realize how all this knowledge will change the world for the better.

Wrapping Up the Walk Through the Past

You will remember and reflect on many ideas, questions, answers, and reinterpretations as you take this walk (literal or figurative) through your past. No two people will have identical memories and experiences, but there's one question that most individuals with AS will be faced with during this process of reflection:

Would it have been better if I had known about my AS when I was a child?

Again, answers will vary. What was the prevailing attitude about the autism spectrum at the time (a question that is very dependent on your age)? Could your family have coped with this? Were the misinterpretations about your behavior positive, or were they negative? GRASP member Jason Zervoudakes summarizes his experience:

Had I known sooner about Asperger's, my relationships with everyone, especially with women, would have been more fruitful. I might have had a family of my own by now.

Yet Heta Pukki, in her article "Telling Peers at School About Asperger Syndrome: Thoughts on How and Why," from the book *Coming Out Asperger: Diagnosis, Disclosure, and Self-Confidence*, states otherwise:

Having seen my credibility sink almost visibly in some people's eyes when they learn about my diagnosis as an adult, I'm profoundly grateful that I was not diagnosed as a child. It could have taken so much energy to fight against condescending attitudes, conscious or unconscious.

For me, it was a mixed blessing that I did not know about my AS. For starters, it was 1973 when my school demanded that my mother get me a psychiatric evaluation. If anything having to do with autism had been identified, it might very well have dictated that I go to the type of school that might have stigmatized me for life. Along with those old report cards, I use this old psychiatric evaluation in many presentations because the observations, to a knowledgeable person today, clearly spell out that I had AS. But in 1973 no one knew about AS. So when it came to the end of the evaluation, the place where they decide *why* you're exhibiting the behaviors they have accurately noted, they got the conclusions very wrong.

To describe what this conclusion was needs some background information: My father had been killed in Vietnam, where he served as a Marine Corps helicopter pilot, and it was an ugly time for everyone. In those years there was an awful lot of passion and emotional baggage being thrown around by everyone in the country, even if they had no personal connection to the war. It felt like I was growing up as a walking outlet for people's emotionally charged opinions, and this contributed mightily to my inability to respect authority figures.

So the conclusion arrived at by the examining professional was that my behavioral difficulties were the result of "emotional problems" caused by my father's death. And while I grew up feeling somewhere inside that this was not true, that I didn't have emotional problems—while I felt the pity others gave me to be excruciatingly condescending, I now see how fortunate I was that they made this mistake. Had those unhappy teachers and all those confused and put-off adults in my life not had something to pity me for, my behaviors would have been interpreted as 100 percent antagonistic with no redeeming value whatsoever. I would have quite simply been thought of as just an arrogant, antisocial kid. The wrath that I suffered from those adults would have been much worse in such a situation.

My personal answer to this question of "Would it have been

better . . ." was based on my circumstances alone, as should yours be based on your personal circumstances.

————————————

THESE reflective walks are never really finished. But hopefully you now have at least some idea of the areas to keep sifting through, as well as a more forgiving filter through which to process your memories. Because it really is true: No one knew.

So what now? Well, now you begin the process of making your life better, armed with a better idea of what needs to be fixed, what you choose to fix, what you choose not to fix, and how to maybe even help others around you understand how good this news can actually be for *them*, as well as for you.

We arrive home from our walk, with work to be done.

CHAPTER FOUR

Disclosure

It is not danger I love. It is life.
—Antoine de Saint-Exupéry, *Wind, Sand and Stars*

———————

Try looking a completely unreasonable person in the eye, and starting with: "I have a neurological condition." What is their reaction? Can you easily think of words to explain further, in such a way that the person will listen and understand, will not think you've gone insane, will not think you're asking for sympathy?
—Heta Pukki, "Telling Peers at School About Asperger Syndrome: Thoughts on How and Why," from *Coming Out Asperger*: *Diagnosis, Disclosure, and Self-Confidence*

Disclosure is common to humanity. Everyone at some time has had to tell someone something about themselves that could have negative consequences in the relationship with that person.

—Stephen Shore, "Disclosure: Talking About What Makes Us Human," from *Coming Out Asperger*: *Diagnosis, Disclosure, and Self-Confidence*

IF someone was dropped into the Arctic High North, the first thing he or she would do is look for another human being. True, some people on the spectrum might become so fascinated by ice crystals, or so disconnected from their bodily signals, that they might fail to recognize the danger inherent in such a scenario. But most people on the spectrum would instinctively seek out a path to their survival. Even if once we find someone we may be more challenged by *what* to say to them, somewhere inside we know that we all need and depend on each other.

Yet we don't just want survival. We want understanding. We want to have our experiences validated. And disclosure is the inexact, arbitrary, and flawed process of revealing to the world that the individual is different, and *why* they are different. It begins a Darwinian journey toward two worlds becoming cognitively indistinguishable as they become more and more able to relate to each other.

Now that you have some sense of what you're processing, the next step is deciding whom to tell, how to tell them, and when to tell them about the diagnosis. Disclosure, at the heart of it, is just sharing. And sharing this information will add to your confidence, will reduce the effects of negative stigma, and might also provide you with fairer, more satisfying circumstances in your life.

The first question is, exactly how public do you want to be about your diagnosis?

Disclosure, like the subject of bullying, has been written about extensively only over the past five years. Led by GRASP luminaries Stephen Shore and Liane Holliday Willey, many new observations and subsequent strategies have surfaced about this risky phase of the post-diagnostic process. But two important facts have been left out of the disclosure literature:

- The strategies almost never work the way you want them to in the short term.

- Many of us with AS have trouble accurately assessing what the rest of the world thinks of us. So how can we expect to make good judgments about how, when, and to whom we disclose?

In my case, probably no one whom I told about my diagnosis responded to my news in a way that left me feeling understood and validated. I felt momentarily let down, even betrayed. However, I see now how unfair it was for me to expect anyone to see all that I could then see and understand, and all that I had been through up to that point. To my pleasant surprise, those "failed" disclosures have proven exceedingly fruitful over the long haul.

We have to understand that unless they were a part of the diagnostic process, the people we tell were probably content with their own ideas about what made us tick. Disclosure can wreck this for them. Even if some people will welcome information that makes so much sense to them, for others, it might obliterate some very comfortable, long-held notions. And the short term *for them* involves having to process an enormous amount of new information. Given time to digest what we've told them, people can come around, especially if the manner in which you disclosed was marked by dignity and courage. Later on, if your life starts to improve because of all that you've learned, and they take notice, they will realize that your diagnosis was probably a good thing. They'll then become more convinced and supportive over time.

But that's a long way off. That short term can indeed be hard. And understanding that it'll take time for the recipients of your disclosure to accept the news, just as it did for you, will provide you with far less disappointment. It will prepare you to be more successful because you won't feel as let down by unrealistic expectations.

The process will also be made easier if you cut yourself some slack should you make a bad decision regarding whom, how, and when to tell. Again, we're at a disadvantage because of the diagnosis itself, which, among other things, can cause us to be overly honest. We have to expect that we will make at least one or two bad choices along the way.

Remember, no matter how many "strategies" there are in all the books available on the subject, disclosure will never be an exact science. What will bring about fulfillment is changing one's expectations of what successful disclosure entails.

For starters, rest assured that you will grow stronger as a result of the disclosure process, from experiencing *failed* disclosures as well as the successful ones.

Possible Consequences of Disclosures

Whether we're on or off the spectrum, we all fear the unknown. So let's start by trying to imagine what's going on inside the head of the recipient of our disclosure: Pretend you're an NT. You're someone who is perfectly content with your assumptions about that friend, employee, or family member who might be a little "off." Then suddenly, that someone asks to speak with you, and proceeds to tell you he has AS. You (the NT) might think, "What the heck is Asperger's syndrome?" You might notice the person disclosing is anxious, and that he's eyeing *you* for what your reaction will be. That'll make you nervous. You might then think to yourself, "Whoa. Too much information. Why is he telling me this?" As a result, you (the NT) might become uncomfortable, and gravitate away from the person with AS—the point being that even when we bravely risk the vulnerable pitfalls of disclosure, we do so by engaging people who might not be so strong themselves.

Furthermore, because of the negative stigma still attached to the diagnosis, you also risk losing credibility with these people as time goes on ("Oh, he won't be able to do this because he has a disability"). Perhaps the expectations others have for you *do* need to be revised because of your diagnosis, and those different expectations will be the bridge to building a better relationship for you both. But more often than not, the expectations don't need to be reduced. You might simply need *accommodation* in order to guarantee what is sought by the outside world.

And while we disclose in order to gain the world's under-standing, we can often instead find belittlement. As Nick Dubin writes in his book, *Breaking Through Hidden Barriers*:

It is hard to develop genuine friendships on the basis of pity alone.

Heta Pukki also, again writing in "Telling Peers at School About Asperger Syndrome: Thoughts on How and Why," from *Coming Out Asperger*: *Diagnosis, Disclosure, and Self-Confidence*, makes a harmless yet startling observation that is actually a consequence of many *successful* disclosures:

It doesn't help to just say it's a disability or a neurological difference if the person receiving this information has no real sense of what that actually means. It's best to be prepared to do a lot of talking.

Why Disclose, and Why Not

Liane Holliday Willey, writing in her essay "Disclosure and Self-Advocacy: An Open Door Policy," from the book *Ask and Tell* (edited by Stephen Shore), speaks many times of her belief in the universal obligation to disclose, citing the greater good that comes from more and more people being forthcoming about who they are. In one particular passage, she states beautifully:

> Neurotypicals see the world through their own eyes, just like we Aspies see the world though our own eyes. That is the nature of humans—to relate to life through individual experiences. But whereas we Aspies have loads of places and people to refer to in order to understand neurotypical behavior, neurotypicals do not have nearly as many autobiographies, movies, novels, textbooks, or even acquaintances, from which they can learn about Aspieland. It is our job, at least it is left to us, to tell—or show—them our needs.

And yet, there is a GRASP member who chooses not to disclose at all because he is a successful partner at a very conservative law firm. Assuming his assessment is accurate that his fellow law partners might react negatively to an AS disclosure, should he then sacrifice his career for the greater good? I think not. I think that while most of us will be in a position to disclose, we still have to adhere to the old adage that you can't help others unless you first help yourself. Having happy lives should be our primary, though not our only, priority.

Holliday Willey again, in her book *Pretending to Be Normal*, provides a list (edited here) of some reasons why disclosure can benefit both the greater collective and the disclosing individual:

- You will not have to be as concerned with concealing, stimming, ticking, sensitivity to sensory input, social confusion, and other AS traits, when you are around those who know, because you will know they realize those actions are often part of AS behavior and, therefore, nothing to take exception to.

- Perhaps when people know you have AS, they will be more supportive if you choose not to volunteer for certain projects that would be too challenging.
- Friends may learn not to expect you to befriend them as they might have otherwise expected.
- When you explain AS to others, you might help them to identify AS in other people they know who have yet to be diagnosed.
- Through educating others and sharing the issues of AS, the chances are you will come to really enjoy and appreciate who you are, no matter how different you may be.

And yet, she cites later in the book how problematic this has often been for her:

I have met some very real prejudices and some very painful misunderstandings on several occasions . . . I wish I could say I understood their reluctance to be open, empathetic and caring, for if I did, I would find peace.

Whom to Tell, and Whom Not

Amid these intimidating back-and-forth arguments about the value of disclosure, we can at least compartmentalize our "who to tell" list into the following categories:

- **Significant others.** I cannot think of any example in which a significant other should not be told. In most cases, the significant other would have been made part of the diagnostic process anyway (most diagnosticians like to consult significant others, if they exist, before granting a diagnosis of AS). In many cases, they also may have been the one who put you on the path toward your eventual diagnosis.

• **Family.** In most cases, you will probably find it appropriate to disclose your diagnosis to family. Perhaps telling every cousin isn't necessary; but parents and siblings usually need to know, as they too can be helped by this information (even if, in the short term, many might react negatively to the news). As stated earlier:
  – The genetic nature of the autism spectrum forces family members to perhaps consider themselves in this same light.
  – There is the possibility that people had you pegged very wrong, may have consequently made some bad decisions for you (or about you), and might now be faced with a lot of guilt and regret—feelings you will want to be prepared for.

• **Friends.** There might be some resistance similar to what family members go through, but by and large this is a friend-by-friend decision based on your assessment of each individual's ability to handle the news. If you decide to disclose to a friend, remember that his response might include a side of him you've never seen. He may have known you were a little different, but maybe he has feelings about "labels"? Remember, again, to give him room despite how much you may desire his immediate acceptance.

• **Employers/colleagues.** On the work front it may be a good, general rule to figure that "if it ain't broke, don't fix it." But in the event that you suspect either your job performance or your interpersonal relations are in a downward trend because of how your diagnosis sets you apart, then disclosure might be a wise move. However, if you are disclosing under the pretext that this will provide you some measure of legal protection, be warned: There are laws about how much protection is afforded, and there are even more misunderstandings about those laws. Even in the case where the laws are on your side, finding a lawyer who will take up your cause can be a dramatically frustrating experience unless you have a lot of money to spend (later in this chapter we'll review the legal landscape in more detail).

• **Religious leaders.** If you regularly attend a church, synagogue, mosque, or temple, it would likely help to have any spiritual guide know about your diagnosis. Furthermore, the strict confidentiality upheld by most religious doctrines regarding such conversations makes this a fairly low-risk disclosure.

• **Doctors and therapists.** As discussed in Chapter 2, individualized therapy is an important tool for handling the many issues faced by those of us with AS. As for medical doctors, even if there are no medical side effects to the individual's diagnosis (such as more dramatically presented sensory or gastrointestinal issues), a physician's confidentiality should be just as trustworthy as that of a religious leader or therapist. And you never know when a doctor will need to know.

Strangers, acquaintances such as shopkeepers you might see every day, neighbors . . . these comprise the more obvious candidates for those who *don't* need to know (legitimate friendships with any of them will have to evaluated individually). But it is safe to say that not all friends, extended family members, professors, employers, and colleagues need to know either.

While I chose to tell certain theatre colleagues, friends, and immediate family members, I did not tell colleagues at the non-profit I represented at the U.N. I felt strongly that, given the politicized atmosphere, not all of them would entrust me with the same responsibilities if they knew I had a diagnosis having anything to do with autism. Looking back, I feel that was a very good call. Yet by not trusting them, there remains the very real possibility that I may have missed an opportunity *for them* to rise up on my behalf, and continue to trust me with the same duties, which would have allowed me an even *more* fruitful relationship with them. Given that my AS had caused me to step on some toes in the past, educating them about AS might have brought about more of an appreciation of my efforts on their behalf, as well as communicating that it was not my intention to disrespect anyone.

How to Tell, and How Not to Tell

Some recently diagnosed individuals experience a strong desire to tell the world in one giant gesture. This seems especially true for those who have endured more problematic relationships in their pasts. The need to have the constant and numerous misunderstandings come to a quick end might compel the individual to send a detailed email to everyone he or she knows.

Such a "one-shot" mass disclosure may feel easier than having to approach people on a case-by-case basis, not only because it saves time, but also because this way you don't have to make decisions about who to tell and who not to tell. You might feel you're destined to fail at making good judgments because of your limited ability at interpreting others—you might be right to think this. But sometimes, there's an off-putting, defiant "If you don't love me for who I am, the heck with you" message that gets conveyed or interpreted this way. The recipients may *want* to be told individually, and may wonder why disclosure was done in such a broad manner. Their ability to receive such news to your satisfaction may indeed be questionable; but if so, they're probably not aware of that. And they'll possibly resent not having been given the benefit of the doubt.

GRASP member Ruth Snyder bravely recounts disclosing in such a uniform manner:

> I first told everyone I knew, family and friends, simply in a Christmas letter by stating, "We have been blessed by Autism, if you want to know more just ask." Of course no one asked.

But can we blame them? As Ruth acknowledges now, this note was too weird for her friends and family. It didn't explain how someone as functional as Ruth could have autism, nor did it explain why she was using a word (*blessed*) that isn't usually associated with autism. Ruth's mistake was in assuming that everyone was as advanced in their thinking and information as she was.

However, there is still much good to be derived from Ruth's declaration. To start, one should approach disclosure with the same attitude as diagnosis—that this is good news, not bad. The information you have holds the potential to clear up just as many mysteries for others as it did for you. Again, we all fear the unknown, and this will be uncharted territory for people if they have never before heard of AS. So you want to sell this diagnosis as a friendly mystery, not a scary one.

Holliday Willey makes many suggestions toward creative disclosure, such as inviting people to local support groups, or using artistic mediums such as slides, video, or art to "tell your story of what AS means in your life" when disclosing. I like this, as people will appreciate the effort and care you put into how you tell them.

Many others suggested that folks on the spectrum should create a business card to give to people: one that, in addition to telling people that the cardholder has AS, will provide a description of what AS is. For encounters with law enforcement or airport security, this can be a good thing to have on hand, depending on where you fall on the spectrum. But personally, I haven't found business cards to be such a good strategy with more typical disclosures. It's just too awkward for the recipient. Make the effort to try and tell people, even if you feel you're not good at explaining things. Any effort will be seen and appreciated by the recipient, even if it takes them time to show it. Tell people individually. Or try to make better decisions about whom to tell. This is more work, yes, and sometimes agonizing work. But the long-term benefit will probably be the respect and understanding you're after. If no appreciation is forthcoming, then your worst-case scenario is that you've discovered someone who is not to be counted on—and that's a good thing, albeit in a sad way: Disclosure often helps us weed out those whom we cannot rely on.

Special Consideration in the Workplace

The work environment carries different rules for disclosure, for oddly enough, you probably need your job more than you need the support of, say, a distant cousin. GRASP member Laura Wysolmierski, a cofacilitator of GRASP's Long Island, New York, network, gives what is easily the best example I've ever seen of disclosing in the workplace. Her situation is unique, and most individuals will not have the circumstances or opportunity to replicate her strategy, but it certainly bears noting:

> I did not formally tell my supervisors and co-workers about my Asperger diagnosis for some time. I felt a little conflicted and ashamed. I did not want to be treated differently. I only mentioned

it to a couple of co-workers I trusted. Then, two years after my diagnosis, I submitted to my employer's newsletter the fact that I was a panelist at a local autism conference, and that I had run my first GRASP meeting. I thought it was time to out myself this way because it was turning what some could consider a negative into a positive. Not long after the newsletter came out, I was made employee of the month. My supervisors wrote about my participation in these two organizations in the declaration.

Wysolmierski's tactic worked on several different levels:

- As she states, it did indeed turn a potential negative into a positive.

- It did so because Wysolmierski's interest in disclosing to her colleagues was somewhat disguised by the fact that it was the newsletter, not just she, that appeared to want to share her story. It was a public acknowledgment that others already found her situation to be compelling and positive enough to publish. This may have gently encouraged others to accept her. She wasn't coming across as needy; she was instead being portrayed as a positive role model—by someone other than herself.

- It spared those around her the awkwardness of being disclosed to, which they probably appreciated. Again: Disclosure can be uncomfortable for both sides.

Another general rule about disclosure in the workplace that Wysolmierski touches on—one that differs from disclosing to family and friends—is that it is almost always to one's advantage to disclose in writing, not in person, at work. Not only does it spare others the discomfort alluded to above, but writing has permanency; and if CC'd to another party in addition to the addressed supervisor, the disclosure cannot be dismissed. If written with what the recipients see as grace, this will only help in securing the sensitivity you're looking for on the job. And in troublesome work environments, written disclosures are what's necessary for the limited legal protections to have any effect.

Is There Legal Protection in the Workplace?

As we've said, not a lot; and what exists isn't ideal. But there is some, and understanding what is available might help you make better decisions about when to disclose on the job.

Currently, the laws that protect the adult on the spectrum are the Rehabilitation Act, specifically Section 504, and the Americans with Disabilities Act (ADA).

Section 504 ("people with disabilities") of the Rehabilitation Act covers only those who are attending schools or working in places that receive federal funding. And the ADA, while more encompassing in that it covers any job where there are at least fifteen employees, is susceptible to state laws and state-by-state sovereignty issues that overrule the federal nature of the law. For instance, in most states, religious organizations are exempt from those laws. They are not held accountable by the ADA whether they have five employees, or five million.

In the workplace, however, as stated earlier under the "if it ain't broke" platitude, it may be time to disclose to a supervisor if you feel your situation at your job is deteriorating because of the social or work constraints posed by your diagnosis. This may not stop the downward spiral. You may encounter more prejudice because of stigma, or people might find it easier to assume that you just want sympathy. Such hurtful thinking is usually an unfortunate sign that they have little desire to accommodate you.

In jobs where there is an already high turnover rate (such as exists in most nine-to-five office jobs), this is especially common as the employing company can then focus on people who "fit in" if they can easily find people who can do the work. But not disclosing in such a situation almost certainly carries worse odds, since any out-of-the-ordinary behavior will go unexplained.

ADA Versus IDEA

Many people who were diagnosed during their school years may be familiar with the protections afforded under IDEA, the Individuals with Disabilities Education Act (a protection that ends after high school). If you remember this, you might wrongly assume that ADA operates under the same assumption. It does not. Whereas IDEA *presumed* your qualifications to be educated, under ADA you must *prove* that you are qualified to be employed.

One of the hardest pills to swallow is that ADA means you can still be fired. "Equal Opportunity," unfortunately, is not the same as guaranteed employment. And the ADA grants people the same equal opportunity as NTs—NTs who often get fired just as frequently as people on the spectrum (NTs just *get* more jobs).

When disclosing in writing to your supervisor, you must describe what it is that you need in order to succeed, *and* you must provide proof that you need it. What this means is that proof of diagnosis is not enough. You'll probably have to go back to a clinician to get him to write something up about your individualized work needs, such as more detailed instructions of the work that is expected of you, or a quieter area to work in. But be advised: A difficulty in getting along with coworkers will not afford you any protection as it doesn't relate to the functions of the job that you are proving you are qualified for.

In situations that appear headed toward unhappy endings,

consulting a lawyer experienced in disability law is never a bad move, and it certainly is better than relying on the brief overview provided here. But what *is* a bad move is licking your chops over a fantasized lawsuit. The legal world does not work the way it does on TV. Overall, you want to stay employed, or concentrate on *switching* jobs rather than quitting them.

When to Tell, and When Not to Tell

Simple. *Don't tell* when you're angry. Try instead to tell when you feel strong, or when you're feeling good about who you are.

Why Is Disclosure So Hard?

It's hard because many individuals on the spectrum have been through experiences that can easily rob them of the strength to withstand the negative fallout of disclosure. The built-up anxiety that the individual goes through prior to making a disclosure takes a lot out of us—regardless of whether or not the disclosure ends up being met with acceptance and understanding.

People might also still doubt that there's anything "wrong" with you, if they feel that up until now you have enjoyed a modicum of success such as a college degree, a steady job, or a relatively normal history with sexuality and/or dating.

You may not even be believed. People might think that your diagnosis is inaccurate, or that you've found a convenient way of not having to adapt by latching on to the latest psychiatric fad. They may feel you are embracing the diagnosis as an excuse to not address your challenges in a manner that others see fit. This will hurt tremendously, for it slams the door (at least for now) on the possibility of their understanding what you've gone through—it is the epitome of adding insult to injury. Even the *idea* that someone would think such thoughts is enough to emotionally drain us, as well as discourage us from future disclosures.

I didn't experience anything so terrible. But I got plenty of funny looks from the theatre colleagues I chose to tell—looks that amounted to "Michael, why are you doing this?" To them, everyone was a little off in the theatre profession, so why not just go with the flow when you sort of fit in due to your unexplained eccentricities. This was a harmless, offenseless response. Yet it still left me feeling invalidated, and somewhat spent as a result because I (unfairly) expected more from them.

We Disclose Because We Can't Go It Alone

In 1919, French composer Maurice Ravel wrote a piano concerto for pianist Paul Wittgenstein, who had lost his right arm in World War I. The concerto was written for only the left hand—a one-handed concerto. To the best of our knowledge, no famous composer had ever written a piece tailored to such a disability before. Nice greeting-card-like story, right? Not quite. It's actually better than that, less condescending too.

Wittgenstein, handicapped or not, had great family wealth, and the composition was commissioned, not donated. Furthermore, Ravel wasn't the only big-name composer Wittgenstein had paid to write such a piece. Richard Strauss, Benjamin Britten, and Sergei Prokofiev had also been commissioned by Wittgenstein, and Wittgenstein wasn't easily impressed. His response to Prokofiev's submission, for instance, was that he didn't understand the composition, and that he therefore wouldn't play it. Wittgenstein didn't want charity. He wanted a composition that suited him, and that respectfully accommodated his abilities. Ravel's piece did exactly that. Even though they later fought, eventually working it out over *how* Wittgenstein was to play the concerto (the more romantic Wittgenstein eventually conceded to Ravel's twentieth-century styles), they worked, argued, and succeeded together out of mutual respect.

In a more well-known case, Jackie Robinson endured trials that are probably beyond our measure of understanding as he broke baseball's color barrier between 1947 and 1949. Most of the players on the other major-league teams didn't want him to succeed, and many of his own Brooklyn Dodger teammates were initially against integrating baseball as well. Before that first season started, a petition was circulated among the Dodger players requesting that Robinson not be allowed on the team. But the Dodgers team captain, shortstop Pee Wee Reese, refused to sign. And Reese's refusal convinced the others to accept, if not welcome, their new teammate. A few months into that 1947 season, when the Dodgers were on the road playing the Reds, the Cincinnati fans began to jeer Robinson relentlessly as he stood at second base. Reese, just a few feet away playing shortstop, went and put his arm around Robinson. The gesture seemed routine—they looked as if they were discussing fielding strategy. But Reese knew exactly what he was doing. He was saying, "I am friends with this man" to everyone in the stadium. The crowd went quiet.

Those examples, in the grand scheme of human history, are but one figurative page out of *War and Peace*. Any society, not just ours, will discourage differences until a few brave individuals have paved the way, and until they show how capable the "different" individual really is. Society only accommodates when they have been shown (not told) the error of their past ways. What Ravel did was tremendous, and it at least led a small group of other composers to follow suit and compose similar works. Reese too, for it made Robinson's glorious road a little less painful. So too was the work of the abolitionists, the freedom riders, and others, even if it was the Wittgensteins, the Robinsons, the Gandhis, and the Kings who had to do the bulk of the work.

Societies progress—that's just what they do. They learn to accommodate everyone as time goes on. They just never do it as fast as we want or need.

We cannot expect the world to understand—even if that world might—but we can expect the world, as we expect family, to try.

Conclusion

Disclosure enlightens the people in our lives, and makes sense of prior mysteries just as the diagnosis does for us. Disclosure helps us venture forth into communities and environments that will indeed accept us for who we are; and helps us leave behind those that won't. Over time, the end result is an increased sense of worth, possibility, and the feeling that the world under your feet has become more certain.

My mother had been a part of my diagnostic process. For both my diagnoses she had been telephoned by the clinicians in order to evaluate my behavioral history. To this day, I don't know whether or not my mother actually *believed* that I couldn't possibly have AS, but I do know that she didn't want me to have it. She clearly indicated in both instances that she expected a verdict of no from the two clinicians. But my gut tells me it was wishful thinking more so than conviction.

The first time I was diagnosed, I called her with the results. I did not notice as I spoke with her how hard a time she was having with the news, and in the midst of a monologue I was giving her, wherein I was sharing how much everything made sense now, she spoke but her voice suddenly trailed off. I heard the whispered words, "I don't think this conversation is going very well," and then for the first time ever, she hung up on me. I failed to see at the time how equally affected she was by this news.

Over time, however, she has become very accepting. She doesn't ask questions about AS (that's not her style), but she constantly applauds GRASP for the work it is doing, and she bombards me with loving affirmations of pride. She probably just needed to know that such a diagnosis wasn't the life sentence of second-class citizenship that she had feared it would be, or that might have been the case during her time. She was also probably terrified by the figurative can of worms my diagnosis may have opened. But sometimes this idea—that getting the diagnosis is good, not bad—is simply a notion that our elders need to see proven rather than explained. She too had built-in prejudices just as I'd had. And while she was always proud of me, she was often confused by me, and as a result, she was made irritable by the confusion. Whether I'm more understandable now to her or not, the acceptance that seems to grow in her every day makes *her* a lot more pleasant to be around as well.

Such a happy ending will not come about because the parent, or whoever, respects and takes pride in you because you have AS. I frankly wouldn't want that as it reeks of condescension. The pride and respect come from how we have *handled* our diagnosis of AS, as well as from a greater understanding of what we have been through prior to our diagnosis.

My mother disappointed me in the short term, yet I am disappointed in myself for that past resentment. This affected her as well as me. That long wait is perhaps the difficulty inherent in many, if not most, successful disclosures. Yet so long as we are prepared, and do not unrealistically expect the world to immediately understand, sympathize, and have read all the same books that we've just read, then our disclosures will be made much easier.

As Stephen Shore states in his memoir, *Beyond the Wall*:

During an encounter with another human, both persons change as a result.

Wittgenstein, Robinson, King, Gandhi . . . they paved roads. But as Ravel and Reese and many others attest, we do nothing great alone.

CHAPTER FIVE

The Right Toolbox: Coping Strategies

Learn the rules so you know how to break them properly.
—The Dalai Lama

———————————

Introduction

FOR those of you who have read other books on autism and AS, you already know that many of them have Strategies sections.

I have mixed feelings about the word *strategies*, because sometimes they just don't work. Like *special*, the word *strategies* has developed a hidden, slightly negative meaning that contradicts its face-value optimism. After a while, these sections and chapters suggest that we're theoretically trying to solve our challenges by talking through them rather than having proven, truly reliable solutions to offer. We don't yet know what will work for everyone.

Strategies do not offer *false* hope, however. They are, in fact, quite useful. But it is often not implied enough that the strategies suggested may not bear fruit. As a result, I've watched many an adult follow the instructions in the Strategies section they were reading, only to emerge with little success, and feel more defeated and distrustful of future advice than is necessary or helpful. We don't have foolproof strategies yet. We have options to *try*.

Should Strategies sections then be ignored or avoided? Absolutely not. Without those options we wouldn't embark on a journey to improve our lives. Readers would be better served, however, if these chapters provided more realistic instructions as to how these strategies should be approached. Eradicating life's obstacles isn't so easy. It involves combinations of ideas, motivations, therapies, luck, hard work, context (such as the person's age and cultural background), and moments of bravery that no book could accurately encapsulate.

Yet (as more than one friend argued) would applying more realistic expectations discourage readers from trying? By adding warnings regarding the anticipated outcomes of strategies, wouldn't we then take away the necessary hope that the strategy will work? Don't we need that hope?

I'd contend no, that we instead need our capacity for hope aimed in a different direction. Instead of needing to believe that the strategy will work, hope instead that you will *not* fall apart if you fail, and fail again; that you will *not* drop in complete anxiety if you are rejected; that you will *not* collapse if someone doesn't like you . . . hope that you really do have it in you to be strong.

I would contend *strategies* are better thought of in quantity, and not quality.

Failure

(Parts of the following four paragraphs are adapted from an article I wrote called "Two Powerful, Wonderful Words . . . 'So What,' " published in *Autism/Asperger Magazine*, July/August 2006.)

Hurt feelings are a part of life, and those on the spectrum probably experience more of these feelings than most neurotypicals. We
often read signals wrong, and we often send signals wrong. We've
therefore been unnecessarily yelled at many times by the time we
reach adulthood. And with each misstep along the way, our discomfort grows, as we ponder the next misinterpretation lurking
around the corner. We know there's that banana peel looming; we
just don't know when we'll slip on it, or how bad the fall will be.

Part of our success in life as adults on the spectrum will be determined by our capacity to reduce our reaction to the criticisms,
taunting, and injustice that many of us face. And as much as I
enjoy talking about how the rest of the world needs to change,
and I do, this is a dilemma where the change has to come from
within ourselves. We have to become better at letting things roll
off our back. We may have been conditioned by protective environments (that we once may have needed) to be too thin-
skinned.

One thing is certain: Few people succeed at anything the first
time out. We all succeed after getting "it" wrong the first few
times. No one I know from my generation has stayed at his first
job—we get better by the sheer momentum of continued trying,
through practice and perseverance, by learning to identify *unnecessary* criticisms, and by caring less and less about them. We
need to feel brave too, not just safe, just like anyone else. Many
of us, dare I say it, need to get tougher.

Ouch! That word! . . . *Tougher*. Another word with connota-
tions more negative than positive. After all, in our past, when
people tried to "toughen" us up, it usually resulted in, at best,
insult and, at worst, irreparable trauma. The gym instructor who
made fun of you, the male relative who awkwardly tried to challenge you yet only ended up destroying your trust in him, the
"language of jerks" . . .

The remedy for such counterproductive insensitivity lies in the salesmanship of the "get tougher" message, rather than in the message itself. Again when helpful information is presented as instruction rather than criticism, there are usually better results for the person with AS.

Now that you've

- been diagnosed

- are aware of the negative stigma facing you

- have walked your walk and reflected on your past

- have made decisions about whom, and whom not, to tell, and

- told them . . .

. . . then you probably now find yourself as someone who to varying degrees (to borrow an expression) is "out." You now face life as someone on the autism spectrum. You may need to initiate, maintain, or repair relationships with other people, and we will look at ways to do that. But we will do so with the idea that instead of spending hours trying to figure out what strategy works for you, you'll try them all. And don't just stop here. Pick up a copy of Zosia Zaks's book *Life and Love: Positive Strategies for Autistic Adults*. Unlike other books that contain Strategies *sections*, Zak's book is three-hundred-plus pages of nothing but strategies.

"Who needs to change now: them, or me?" is a question that most people at this stage of the diagnostic process will be asking. The answer is, of course, "Both," but as we learned from Sigmund Freud, if you want someone else to change, then *you* have to change.

What to Change Is Your Choice

Whether the conversation is sports, dating, or employment, you could arguably boil every dialogue at any GRASP support meeting down to the question of "When do I assimilate (to the rest of the world's ways of doing things) and when do I not?" Digesting this notion of choosing, and making choices—rather than feeling like the choices are being made for you—is essential to your future success. GRASP tries its best to be about choice. For when it comes to decisions about assimilating into mainstream society, our philosophy is not to push people into making one choice over another. Some people want the American dream, others want to be left alone to be who they are, and no judgment of either side by the other will benefit anyone.

For example: Say someone has a true hatred of wearing ties. There may be sensory issues that make the person feel like he's being choked, or perhaps the particular cloth of a dress shirt makes him feel awful. Well, let's say this person wants a certain job very badly, but he'd have to wear a tie every day if he got it. GRASP may have suggestions to help the individual on the long road of breathing techniques, relaxation exercises, or yoga—whatever—that'll help him become able to wear ties, if (and this is a big "if") he chooses to undergo all that hard work. Well, let's imagine this person saying, "You know what? I want that job. I deserve it. I'm going to bust my bottom to do the work it takes to be able to wear a tie." In this case the individual has made a choice that should be supported, respected, and given the opportunity to succeed.

Someone else, however, if presented with how much work it'll be, may opt instead to say, "You know what? I'm just too tired. I've been through too much trauma because of all this stuff relating to my Asperger's, and I just don't have the strength to

There is much division in the autistic peer community about conforming or not, and very little of it is positive. It mostly revolves around conforming being "better" than not conforming, or vice versa, rather than focusing on choice and everyone having the informed opportunity to choose. GRASP fights very hard for people's right not to have to conform, for such pressure can often be society's attempts to subconsciously demonize or denounce so-called autistic behaviors.

But so too should no one criticize the choice of someone on the spectrum to advance in the world through assimilation. To tell someone else not to try and have a family, or pay college bills, or own a house—which often is telling someone to be poor—is the farthest thing from any notion of what community entails. Sadly, misery does indeed love company. We must instead respect each other's choices.

---

learn how to get that tie around my neck. I choose to just be who I am, even if it means not getting that job." That person too has made a choice that is his alone to make. Without the belief that this was his choice, he might instead feel that others had *denied* him that job, or maybe that the world was out to get him—that he'd been robbed. As a result, he would be bitter.* But if he accepts the notion of choice, then he always will have the option of choosing otherwise in the future—a choice that is his, and not the feeling that he's acquiescing to unwanted pressure.

Hopefully by now you're beginning to get an idea as to where in your life, if anywhere, you'd like to make changes. In other words, you're making choices based on who you are and what you personally want out of life. The best helpers will be the

---

* If the individual is still bitter, then additional therapy is needed to help him realize that he is more empowered than he thinks.

books you read, the articles you download, or the videos you watch, for these will help you cognitively understand what sets you apart. Becoming your own expert, your own advocate, not only boosts your confidence, but without understanding who you are, you might continue on in the semidoomed vein of assuming you are something that you are not. Again: "Pretending to be normal," to quote the title from Liane's book, probably makes for more trouble than the diagnosis itself. And at the time of this writing, there were no social skills, job skills, or sexuality curriculums yet for adults on the spectrum. There are plenty for children, and hallelujah, some curriculums for teens have been spotted recently (that don't just teach an action, but also explain *why it might be advantageous to do it*). But as an adult, you will have to be the repair person, the mechanic, the doctor. And again, now that you know what you have, you won't be using the wrong toolbox to make those repairs.

Which repairs are needed depend on who you are, and how bravely you can admit to what your strengths and challenges are.

Which repairs you *want* to make are up to you.

First, Focus on You

Before we get to strategies having to do with your family, work life, significant others, and so forth, let's take from that Freud quote and focus on you.

Environmental Changes

Let's start with your room, or your apartment or house. Are you comfortable in it? Is it filled with things that make you feel supported, with books you like, pictures you enjoy (consider, if your room had a personality, would it like *you*)? Do you like clutter, or do you like cleanliness? Do you like cleanliness but hate to clean, and therefore need to find the strength to change your habits about cleaning; or find the money for a cleaning person?

Get in touch also with whatever sensory integration issues you may have—for example, visual distaste for fluorescent lighting, audio difficulties with processing certain sounds, aversions to certain smells—then change your living space to accommodate them. Whatever aesthetic criticism you might open yourself up for from would-be interior designers pales in comparison to the discomfort or anxiety these sensory overloads may cause. Make your living space—and if you can, your work space—function primarily for you, not for others.

Of course, once you leave that space, your sensory integration issues are suddenly at the mercy of others. Still, even in areas where your sensory issues are not accommodated, you are not without empowering weapons. Zaks offers a great list in her book—a "sensory emergency kit"—that you can always carry with you if need be:

- Sunglasses, to shade your eyes from the light
- Walkman, earplugs, or noise-cancellation earphones to drown out sounds
- Personal filtration mask to filter out smells
- Snacks/drinks in case you are away from home and can't find any tolerable food or drink
- Gum or candy in case you try a new food or drink and the taste is horribly unpleasant
- Distraction items such as little games, toys, puzzles, or a pad of paper and a pen to soothe or calm yourself if you are very anxious, or have to wait a long time

- Tactile items such as something interesting to hold, squish, or roll in your hands if tactile stimulation soothes you
- Extra clothing if you are hypersensitive to air-conditioning or have other temperature issues

Pets

It's been fairly well proven that pets provide stress relief for almost everyone. Yet in addition to that obvious benefit, many well-known authors on the spectrum have demonstrated heightened abilities to communicate with animals. Whether this is due to a true, preexisting talent at kinetically understanding animals, or whether our relative inabilities at relating to peers have driven us to put more effort elsewhere, many people on the spectrum have conveyed or shown feelings of connection with a variety of animals. Temple Grandin has made a career of combining engineering skills with her insight into the mind-set of cattle. Jerry Newport frequently writes lovingly of the many birds that roam around his home. Liane Holliday Willey has long connected with horses. Dawn Prince-Hughes discovered herself through her relationship with the gorillas she works with. Jim Sinclair, author of the landmark 1993 article "Don't Mourn for Us," doesn't just swear by service dogs as do many others on the spectrum, he also trains them. Lastly, a myriad of GRASP members seem to love their cats to disproportionately passionate levels.

If you can handle the responsibility (and that's a big "if"), this is something to think about. I had three dogs from 1975 to 2004, all of whom gave me companionship and lessons in responsibility, especially in my younger years. And this provided me with something akin to a social safety net. However, I should honestly relate that my deep need for these dogs receded dramatically once I became a father. Now a father of two (and owing somewhat to living in a big city such as New York), I am more than content being temporarily petless.

Your Body

In going through actor training in college, I frustrated many teachers. I couldn't get my body under control. They chastised me for "weird gestures" that they felt I was superimposing over my acting. And it annoyed me that I wasn't able to take their direction as well as my classmates. Believe me, I was trying. The good part (aside from getting cast in some awesome roles where the characters were lunatics) was that despite the relative inadequacy, *I got better*. I ironed out many of my motor skills issues that separated me from others. And I got better because someone was honestly telling me what I looked like.

In part, what those teachers were telling me hurt my feelings. But I knew (or I chose to see) that my feelings were of less consequence when compared with the bigger picture of what I wanted out of life. Their observations allowed me to see what I never would have seen myself.

If there isn't an acting class available to you, find a way to videotape yourself. Most digital cameras have the ability to take at least thirty-second movies, so see what you look like compared to others, and then practice in front of a mirror if you want to make changes. You could ask a trusted friend to be a second set of eyes, and if you wanted to be very meticulous, you could also keep a journal of your progress.

If you feel you would like more fluctuation of tone in your voice, try taping scenes on television where there is lots of dialogue, and practice copying the inflections used as you watch the tapes. You could also see a speech therapist, or take a speech class. And if there *is* an accessible acting class nearby, that'll help too.

Do you have a friend who's admired for the way he or she dresses? If so, ask that friend to help you to pick out some new clothes. In my early twenties, I had a wardrobe of about five pairs of Levi's and twenty plain white T-shirts. That was pretty much all I wore. I looked okay, and because it was the first outfit I'd found that people thought looked okay, I wore it every day. Luckily, my eye for clothing improved somewhat with age. But even then, while I later could dress up and dress down, I still didn't have an "in between" look. (I still don't, but I'm lucky now to have a wife who picks out every stitch I own.)

Ditto for grooming hints. Ask someone you trust. Hair, facial hair, ear hair, nose hair—whether you need just a snip here or there, or whether you are unaware of any issues of odor that need to be resolved—wherever you are on the spectrum, there may be improvements to be made. Bravely asking, instead of trusting your assumptions, may surprise you with the information it reveals. And though the new information (if there is any) might be embarrassing to hear, addressing those needs will offer you a better chance at improving your circumstances.

And before you set out to change every aspect of your behavior, looks, and style, try to find the silver lining in how you look and act right now.

Think, for example, of the occasional AS trait of talking to ourselves. Personally, I've talked to myself my entire life. I hide it fairly well in that I engage in the practice more when no one's around. But every once in a while I get sloppy and am "caught," and this particular behavior scares some people. It has traditionally been thought of as an indication of dementia, one that our culture has always made fun of, or has attributed to madness. But unless I'm deluding myself, I've learned that what I'm doing when I talk to myself is actually quite positive. I'm usually working "stuff" out. I'm maybe rehearsing a conversation that I think will happen, or I'm preparing myself for some upcoming challenge. Many a time have friends seen me and stated, laughing: "Michael, I tried calling out to you on the street the other day, but boy, were you out of it. You just walked on and talked to yourself . . ." In these situations I've learned to respond by saying something like, "Hey, sorry about that [then I laugh with them], I guess I was really spaced out," though what I really want to say is:

"Excuse me, do you know how much work I got done?"

Your Health: Physical and Emotional

In effective communication, the signal from the sender is clear, and the receiver is open and receptive to hearing it. Becoming aware of our emotions and honestly communicating them is the groundwork of sending clear signals.
—Ruth Elaine Joyner Hane, "Communicating Through Advcacy and Self-Disclosure: Four Ways to Connect," in *Ask and Tell* (Stephen Shore, Editor)

Reducing anxiety not only feels great, it also alleviates many noticeable behavioral differences. So reduce away. Exercise will do more than just help you to feel and look better; it also helps you breathe better, and feel more centered where you are at any given time. It helps you iron out motor skills issues, and it leaves you feeling empowered as you start to notice the startling positive difference that exercise makes in your life. Breathing exercises found in any book on actor training can help in this area as well, as can the aforementioned yoga class. And while finding inner peace is right for some, finding an empowering form of exercise such as karate, judo, tae kwon do—even boxing—can be of enormous positive impact and shoot your confidence levels through the roof.

There are many things you can do to help both your body and your mind.

Eat Right

Take the time to eat properly. Too often many of us fall in love with fast food—not just with the accessibility, but also the soft and safe textures of fast food (especially the burgers). The high-fat content of most fast food makes this a very poor way to eat. Again, when you feel better physically, you feel better elsewhere in ways you have to experience to understand.

Make the Most of Music

Music can paradoxically be both the most overstated, yet still underestimated influence on our lives. Anytime I've endured or witnessed a stressful event, I have run to music the way others do to a medicine cabinet. Music therapy, a more formal approach than merely throwing a CD on, can be an enlightening introduction to this world, as can an art therapy class or session.

Get More Connected to Your Sense of Right and Wrong

If your sense of moral expectations doesn't seem to connect with the rest of the world's, read books on ethics. Ethics break down morality and moral expectations in ways that may make more sense to you.

Or read books on philosophy. These can be incredibly beneficial because of one particular, guiding rule of philosophy—that there are no answers, only deeper questions. This absence of "yes or no" conclusions is advantageous to the average spectrumite as it reduces our very Aspergian need for absolutes (and further helps us to understand the concept of letting go). Both ethics and philosophy can better explain ambiguous and vague interpretations of how the world works to those with more mathematically and scientifically suited brains—yet without shutting out the creative mind.

Look Deeper at Your Emotional Self

And if you are still feeling distanced from your own emotions, reading about how emotions themselves work, as well as how people erroneously *think* they work, can often help you find and fine-tune into those emotions for the first time. Martha C. Nussbaum's *Upheavals of Thought: The Intelligence of Emotions* is not an easy read. The book contains more than seven hundred pages of dense writing, and there may be better-suited books out there that cover the same topic. But I mention it out of prejudice in that it is one of the best books I've ever read (even if I would never pretend to fully understand it). It clarifies how emotions are often not the irrational forces we think they are, but instead, they can be fueled by surprising wisdom.

As Nussbaum says in her book with reference to so much of what we've discussed:

> In fear, one sees oneself or what one loves as seriously threatened.
> In hope, one sees oneself or what one loves as in some uncertainty
> but with a good chance for a good outcome . . . these emotions
> embody not simply ways of seeing an object, but beliefs.

Dr. Elizabeth Kübler-Ross identified the well-known five stages of grieving* and led the emergence in this country of the hospice movement (wherein people die under infinitely more sensitive and humane conditions). She realized through her work with the dying that our emotions were far better protected by being brave enough to become emotionally involved. She found, through trial and error, that burying emotions took more out of a person than expressing them did.

In our own minds, imaginary illnesses can seem real, just as unsolicited internal praise can lift us. And yet, our thoughts do not have such an effect on the rest of the world. That is why it is so true, rather than being a pretty thing to say, that we can only truly control ourselves, or our *approach* to the outside world; for we cannot control the outside world itself. This is often the unexpected, never anticipated road that leads to that oft-desired outside change. Improving your lot on your own, needing the outside world's approval less and less as things get better for you, will then effectively *lead* that outside world through your example (again, it's the difference between "show" and "tell"). It will then change. That's not "self-help," feel-good spin. That's real.

Strategies for Family Interactions

Give Them Space

Remember, you're not the only one affected by your diagnosis. Parents, grandparents, siblings, even uncles, aunts, and cousins

---

* In order of occurrence, they are denial, anger, bargaining, depression, and finally, acceptance. We experience these five stages every day, whether or not a close loved one dies, or whether our scoop of ice cream has fallen onto the ground.

will be affected by this news. Most of them probably didn't ask you to get evaluated: That was probably your decision, and no matter how good a decision it was, this is news many of them might not have asked for. If they cannot be there for you in a supportive manner right away, they may be able to later. If this is the case, let them be. Leave them to "walk their walks" and hope for the best.

Human beings have an incredible urge to make judgments before any true comprehension takes place. We make assumptions— that's how we live, and this is too human a characteristic to expect it to ever change. And although we may be experiencing more pain brought on by *others'* misassumptions, we on the spectrum are no exception. Because of our missing elements tied to nonverbal communication and social norms, we can "misassume" even more.

Families will have immediate things to say about your diagnosis when you disclose it to them. They might have words for you that make sense, and they might have words that originate only from fear. And we who rely so much on text are, therefore, wise to understand that language is used to cover up, even lie, just as much as it is used to reveal truths. Do not take hurtful words from such family members too much to heart. The hurt is likely unintentional.

Your degree of success at being able to let things roll off your back will be determined in part by how much independence you have in your life. For the person who relies on family for day-to-day things (for car rides, for a roof over your head, and so on), this process will be harder. For the spectrumite who lives independently (and therefore knows he can separate whenever he wishes), this process will be easier.

But handling family members who are disturbed by this process is never easy. Initially, and for a while thereafter, relatives may be embarrassed, depressed, or disappointed. As Holliday

Willey's mother once told her, "The truth may set you free, but it doesn't necessarily set everyone else free." People will have emotional reactions, but emotional reactions dissipate. They do not last forever.

My friend Simon (the Jesuit priest mentioned earlier) taught me something else besides the first step in life being to find a community. He once told me a great story from the life of the Buddha, one that relates to families, especially parents. As best as I can recall the story, the Buddha, it turns out, was born to well-off parents, a king and queen, in fact. Once those in charge of his care noticed how capable of compassion this son was, they began to fear for him. So they built walls around their home, and they built him palaces. This way the Buddha would experience the pleasures of luxury, and would therefore not see all the sick and poor people who dominated life outside their walls.

Well, of course we know that the Buddha must have gotten out; otherwise, he wouldn't have become the Buddha. But what is sometimes lost in the telling of the story is how much the Buddha's family loved him.

Families may not be ready for all that you have learned, and for all that you have to say. Initially, no one in my family was either. Your restraint may save *you all* from the frustration of hurtful comments.

If Things Aren't So Good: Walk Away for a While

Family does indeed have that potential to give us superhuman strength, and yet drag us through the mud. Family is also a constant, for better or for worse, one that will exist throughout our lives. And if their reaction to your new ways of living, or looking at life, is unsupportive (or worse, destructive), to the best of your ability it would be wise to walk away for a while.

If you have been able to blend in with the rest of the world more successfully than most adult diagnosees, then your family might display some denial or resentment. If you have some significant challenges that, though not properly identified until now, have caused concern, or that have stretched the family's resources or energy, there may be too much frustration for them to be glad that you have finally found the right road. They may simply be lamenting, "Oh great, another label . . ." with great cynicism.

In what has to be a very personal decision, there are some relationships that either can't be fixed, or the effort needed for repair is just too costly. When I was growing up, and certain relatives, neighbors, or teachers were really having a hard time with me (or more truthfully, really didn't like me), without knowing it I had a choice. I could have either kept going back to them, wanting their approval, and repeatedly asking, "What am I doing wrong?" in so many ways, over and over again. Or I could have walked away from them.

Something inside me told me that I didn't have the power or the ability to fix things with these folks. I realized that I wasn't good at doing what they wanted, or behaving in a manner they were trying to steer me toward. And furthermore, as best as I could figure these situations out (and I had plenty of misreads), *I didn't agree* with their criticisms. To their dismay, I really liked myself. I wasn't *certain* I was right to think this, but my gut told me I'd be better for it. And so I let go of those failed relationships, interpreting them to be out of my control. And I instead went looking elsewhere for good relations—often, granted, to run into the same problem over and over again. But I always felt more in command of my life as a result of having *acted*, of having relied on *myself* for a solution, rather than on them. This inadvertently strengthened my tolerance for failure.

For some of us, this loss may be more painful (such as a parent) or less painful (such as the distant cousin). But if that person is just so frustrated by you that he can't listen to what this new discovery means about you, and your relationship with him, then you should instead spend the time finding relations that are healthier, and mutually reciprocal. Based on the unknown variables going on inside the other person, to do otherwise is often to admit faults about yourself that might not exist. Furthermore, the act of separating may be the jolt he needs to recognize how important this moment really is for you. Family members have perhaps gotten used to your needing them—needing their opinions, and their approval. Remember, they too may be too mired in past frustrations to be able to reach the part of themselves that *is* capable of handling your news.

Many of you may still live with your family as adults. For you, this will be the hardest because you really can't go anywhere. The solution is to try and change exactly that. Even if you endure great challenges because of your diagnosis, investigate supportive housing options, low-cost housing that is government-subsidized such as Section 8 housing (and despite any difficulties with family members, you may need to ask for their help with the application procedures). If you have friends, or a therapist that you trust, check in with them as to whether such a move is advisable, but really pursue the idea with them even if there's some initial pessimism (at the beginning of such a conversation they may simply be scared for you). If you can pull off such a dramatic change in your life, you may not end up living in as nice a place as your family provides. But almost no one lives in a nice place when he or she first leaves home. That's kind of the point: to grow into your own space, and labor for *your own* improvements. If you cannot drive, investigate public transportation, or look into ride services (New York, for instance, has a program called "Access-a-ride"). Or ask acquaintances nicely, so as not to possibly make yourself a burden, "Hey, next time you're going to the supermarket, could I go with you? I don't drive and it gets really difficult for me to shop because of that." Ask more than one acquaintance if you can, so as not to burden one friend with the responsibility of making sure you have food to eat. And if you have less money for food because of moving out, this too is symptomatic of everyone else when first leaving home. It's sort of a ritual we all go through so take pride in it. It means you're on your own.

If Things Are Better: Invite Them In

Is your family ready? Do they see what good news this really is? Did it take two days, or two decades? Either way, be graceful in how you teach them. Now you're working *with* them. Let go of any lingering resentments. Don't accost them with statements like, "I told you so," or "See what you did to me?" to make them feel worse about past mistakes simply because you now have the opportunity. Instead, just let them into your world, checking with them periodically to make sure they get breathers in between the blasts of potentially overwhelming revelations that you unknowingly might be presenting them with.

What does this mean in practical terms? Well, obviously it means telling them what you're going through, and how your world is changing because of your diagnosis. But it also could mean sharing books that have helped you understand what all this means, perhaps bringing them to a support group, or helping them to find a parents support group of their own. Maybe this includes introducing them to others who have helped you to process this information, so that your family members can get an outsider's take on how wonderful this diagnosis has been for you.

You have an enormous amount to show and teach now, insight that could truly benefit them. This information might validate their long-standing worries that "there was something out of the ordinary going on" with you—a hunch they had, though one that their friends and acquaintances didn't believe. This information might also make them realize that they weren't bad parents, for even if there is regret at not having known prior—if there is guilt (which is simply what parents may have to experience despite the mountains of evidence citing their blamelessness)—they will now be able to own up to what really caused the more questionable moves they once made on your behalf. Usually the answers surround well-intentioned, unavoidable, and forgivable ignorance, and not the more stigmatic notion of faulty parenting.

Treat carefully too the idea that some of them may share the diagnosis. In the case of (for instance) a long-institutionalized relative who may have been confined under misdiagnosis . . . disclose your feelings about that person being on the spectrum because that person could be greatly helped. *That's* the dramatic example that is the exception, and not the rule. The rule should be to let them (especially parents) *ask* you where you think you got your AS from. Once they start to learn about AS, they may (or may not) see a genetic link, and they may be very uncomfortable with the idea, whether it's them or someone else. But that's their walk to walk, not yours.

If there are bumps in the road, stay on the road. Such bumps will happen, and these moments are very different than those with relatives who clearly want nothing to do with the news. Again, you're working with friends now. You're guiding people who are bravely trying to see with fresh eyes. Reward that bravery with kindness and patience. Otherwise they could suffer a setback and stop being brave very quickly.

GRASP's Manhattan group witnessed such a bump. A mother in her fifties once accompanied her recently diagnosed twenty-eight-year-old son to his GRASP meeting. She started to ask the group some questions as to why her son thought the way he did in certain situations. The son would try to answer, but she wouldn't let him speak. She instead wanted to hear what the group had to say. As things continued on in this way, the son continuously trying to interject, she got more and more frustrated. Finally, she blew up, and yelled, "But everything he says is so stupid!"

The twenty to twenty-five people in the room suddenly rose and shouted her down not only for the error in her thinking, but also for having said it in her son's presence (in a parent support group, away from her child, such a statement might reluctantly be considered an appropriate outburst). I could have stopped the lengthy reprimand, but I purposely let the group chew her up a little bit before calling them off. She needed the figurative spanking, and the empowerment demonstrated by the group made me tremendously proud.

And to that woman's heroic credit, she was back at the next meeting, listening intently, and quietly.

Revisiting Apologies

Having a child with Asperger's Syndrome can change the parents' social life, conversation and atmosphere at home. Social contact can be reduced to repeatedly having to explain and to apologize for the child's unusual behavior. Conversations become pedantic and dominated by the child's interruptions and questions, and the household becomes regimented so as not to distress the child by too much change.

—Tony Attwood, *Asperger's Syndrome*

Some parents must be thinking, "I've been apologizing for my kid all my life, and now I'm supposed to apologize *to* him?" You, in turn, may be wondering if it is appropriate for you to apologize to your parents for whatever they may have gone through.

I don't think it is necessary to apologize to your parents. While they may have done nothing intentionally wrong, by having AS *you simply did nothing wrong.* Period. Both sides may have wronged each other via mutual frustration and the antagonism that often grows out of that frustration, but I know as a parent that I chose to have a child. I chose to bring someone, now two children, into this world, and that meant committing myself to all that my child would eventually bring me. It doesn't mean my boys will never hurt me, nor does it mean I am any better a parent than the next person. But my eldest's AS is simply not something he did wrong, or even right. I owe him everything I can give him. If he cracks up my car, he will perhaps owe me an apology. But for having AS? No. Even if you *want* to tell your family you're sorry for what circumstances brought them (as opposed to any personal responsibility on your part), doing so might contribute to the internal idea that you are, or were, a burden to them. Your diagnosis in an unaccommodating and unaware world might have placed burdens on them, but you yourself did not.

Apologies are rarely appropriate. But when they are appropriate (such as in repairing damage from hurtful, angry outbursts), and if done correctly, there can be magic; restoration of full yet buried love, the likes of which may leave you breathless because you never had a chance to see that love in full bloom, unhampered by years of accumulated frustrations.

Forgiveness is less complicated than the act of apologizing: You don't need another party to implement forgiveness, you can do it on your own; and because of that, forgiveness can be applied with far less mental anguish. But both acts carry incredible power.

Remember that our temptation will always be to tell it like it is. Some families might be aided by the forthrightness inherent in this tendency. But others might not be ready for brutal honesty. Love without truth definitely does lie, but truth without love can often do more harm.

Strategies for the World of Work

Choosing a Career and Getting a Job

Much has been written on the subject of what jobs are appropriate for people with AS; the consensus being that the best professions are those that rely more on solitary work, work where there is some system of logic, creativity, and where the work atmosphere is more behaviorally permissive and less socially demanding. At the top of the list of jobs to be avoided are positions dealing with sales or customer service. Again, though, these suggestions are based on probability, and not the very real possibility that you may be able to handle any job that exists.

Also, you can spend tons of time outlining what your skills are, how good you really are at them, and where you need improvement, but you'll still be at the mercy of the job market you live in, and whether or not you can navigate the social realities of a particular workplace. Dr. Brenda Smith Myles, who has researched the lives of people with AS as much as anyone, found something very alarming in one study—that only 2 percent of those with AS *who are employed* are employed in the field in which they were trained (I know I'm certainly not in the field that reflects my degree). When we consider how few people on the spectrum are actually employed, this doesn't bode well for putting a lot of hope into finding the perfect job.

You should still know what you want to do, and what you can do, what your interests are, what your capacity for multi-tasking is . . . but it would help to be flexible, and especially understand that you can still look for the ideal job while you're employed in a job that isn't particularly suited to your strengths. Usually, in order to pay the bills, we need *any* job at any given moment. And few people land their ideal job the first time someone hires them.

Even if "the perfect job" is unattainable, the search itself should find you in a better job as your career moves along. But keep in mind that the perfect fit won't merely reflect your interests, abilities, and level of social challenge. The perfect job will cater to the different ways you might learn, your sensory capacity, and it will also allow you to grow both personally and professionally. The future question of "What would happen at this job if I disclosed?" might also be wise to consider. So dream, and labor away—but letting go of the idea that you'll hit that perfect gig the first time out will serve you well.

Another issue compounding workforce problems is that most of the colleges that train us take little responsibility for teaching the social skills necessary on the job. Universities might rightfully argue that this isn't their place, but the reality is that without informing students that they might suffer socially, colleges are indeed shortchanging their spectrum students as they hand them a degree. For embedded in such an act lies a silent, unfair promise that academics are all we need, an unspoken assurance that doesn't fly outside the safe confines of university life.

Much has also been written about the interview process, and no strategy will fit everyone. But reductions in anxiety, a belief in yourself and your abilities, and the capacity for understanding when to listen, and not talk, are crucial to your success. Understand too that, if you don't get the job, you can set yourself up very nicely for future positions if you perform well in the interview.

Others knowing you is often imperative, and that's why everyone under the sun may have already told you to "network." *Network* is another word for socialize, I know. But the more of this you can do, the better. It's a mathematical truth that your chances are increased the more people you know, the more people who know about you, and who either like or respect you.

If you're simply having no luck at landing a job, but you truly believe you can do the work, one way to network and show your skills is to volunteer at a company you would like to work for. Volunteering allows you to safely meet other people. It can also help to perhaps override any doubts people might have had about your on-the-job abilities. The only problem is, of course, that you're not being paid, but if the point is to convince them to pay you, and you can swing the temporary lack of funds, it may be worth your while to offer your services in this capacity. However, if you've been there a year and they still don't want to hire you for real, it's time to go. Find another company to volunteer with.

Strategies on the Job

Learn from my personal mistakes outlined in Chapter 3: Get to know what the boss wants. The way things make sense to you might be misleading. If you're even the slightest bit unsure as to how the place operates, ask and ask again, until, of course, you start to see that the boss is getting a little tired of your questions.

Roger N. Meyer wrote an enormous book on the whole employment world for people with AS. His *Asperger Syndrome Employment Workbook* contains a significant list of challenges possibly faced by the average spectrumite. Some of the more notable selections from his list are:

- Difficulty handling relationships with authority figures
- Difficulty in receiving and giving criticism and correction
- Low level of assertiveness (*although I would contend we have the capacity for the opposite problem as well*)
- Reluctance to ask for help or support
- Problem accepting compliments, often responding with self-deprecating or quizzical comments

Finding polite ways to request accommodations will also serve you well. Getting flustered and telling people you have to have that quiet room won't score you any points, and can usher in the beginning of the end if you don't successfully apologize and contain yourself in the future. Learn how to convey a not-so-nice feeling nicely. As Lynne Moxon points out in an essay more geared toward sexuality, "Diagnosis, Disclosure and Self-Confidence in Sexuality and Relationships," from the book *Coming Out Asperger: Diagnosis, Disclosure, and Self-Confidence*:

There is more than one way of saying no.

When I entered the workforce out of school, I did not think I needed to learn any rules about socialization. I thought that if I excelled at the work, I would be fine, even more than fine. I was wrong. You have to learn those rules. It stinks, but you have to learn them, and they will be different at every job you'll ever have. Still, once you learn them, your confidence will have you feeling incredibly good about yourself. And the more you can see the benefit in learning them, the more you will learn them.

Manage those emotions too. Don't be too much of a perfectionist. Understand that competition is natural. And when you lose, lose with dignity, brush it off, and let it go. That shows others that you can work with them. Don't be sarcastic with the boss, even if it's okay to be sarcastic with coworkers every once in a while. Don't butt into other people's work too often, and if you're someone with more significant challenges, no tantrums or meltdowns. Find a way to hide it, excuse yourself, and go let it out elsewhere, such as at a gym, or on your walk home.

Two years after diagnosis, my relationships have been more civil towards [my coworkers]. I believe they improved because I learned to be easier on myself and others for our imperfections.

—Jason Zervoudakes

Scattered amid these pages are many suggestions. Sadly, they're somewhat useless without a realistic assessment of the work environment you find yourself in. Should you be fired (most people get fired at least once, myself included), treat it as a setback—one that you can learn from—but get right back out there. Maybe you screwed up, maybe you got screwed, maybe you were simply misunderstood, and maybe the job simply wasn't a good fit for you. But just as this book asks you to assume control over so much, it also asks you to know where and when you have no control whatsoever. The days of working for one company your whole career are pretty much over, and that's for everyone. You will likely bounce from job to job just like so many others do. All you can do is your best.

Strategies for Meeting People, Dating, Managing an Existing Relationship, and Having a Healthy Sex Life

Some Good News

Back when I was a kid, the movies portrayed geek types as destined to be alone. Jokes (some cruel, some not so cruel) were made in fictional books, plays, and television toward the socially challenged characters. And at best, the (usually) bespectacled side character was supposed to just endure the ribbing in the "good-natured" context in which it was supposedly given. It was even rarer for this type of character to end up with a mate at the end of the story.

These days, not only are such characters ending up in today's narratives with a soul mate, but their search for a significant other is often the lead story. In short, the cerebral activity—the smarts— or even just the special interests of these characters can now be thought of as attractive. And one could very well argue that the prevalence rates have minutely increased because, God forbid, as these attitudes travel, *we're procreating more*. As society becomes more and more fascinated by either academic excellence or behavioral differences, the shift from repulsion, to condescension, to respect has resulted in unions, and subsequent offspring.

Much of what you take away from this section will depend on your level of challenges, your cultural and/or religious beliefs, and whether you are trying to find, or maintain, relationships. Just as GRASP has people from many places on the spectrum, many cultures, many sexual orientations, and many political backgrounds, GRASP also has members with vastly different hopes and dreams for their love lives. Some of GRASP's members are happily married, some have children, and many others have never been on a date. Some members are, or hope to be, very sexually active, some have no desire for premarital sex, and in both cases, as discussed in Chapter 3, the level of sexual appetite will vary. Amid so many variables, readers should take what they will from the following and try to maintain a sense of pluralism as they read.

Meeting People

Do you wish to meet people? If so, where are you looking? If you watch a lot of TV, you've probably got the idea that we all meet significant others a lot in bars, at parties, or through friends and colleagues. Yet going to parties requires us to withstand the sensory challenges of noisy, crowded gatherings, as well as having friends to invite you in the first place. Bars too are suspect because they require meeting strangers often without an intermediary to introduce you (such as you might find at a party). And as a substitute for such a go-between, people at bars meet one another through the use of nonverbal communication: winks, nods, and other physical signals that not a lot of us with AS are all that great at.

Have you tried the Internet? Many people report a lot of successful relationships that began on the Internet, and it does seem to be a far safer venue than it used to be many years ago, when predators operated without any restrictions. Still, be careful: The predators aren't all gone, and on the Internet it's possible for people to lie about who they are, sometimes in dangerous ways.

The golden rule is to do as much as possible. Get outside. As far as your social challenges will let you, go to singles events, attend church gatherings, join softball teams, take cooking classes, and the like. As in employment, volunteering can be a wonderful opportunity, especially if you're volunteering at something that you're passionate about. Part of where we have a legitimate shot at someone being attracted to us lies in that ability to bury ourselves in work that we love and believe in—and then being seen doing it. So find some of that work, and if you sense that in this capacity there's no one there for you at your present volunteer position, move on. Volunteer somewhere else, and keep trying until you have some luck.

For the record, I rarely had luck at "blind" encounters. I needed some semblance of a reputation, or someone seeing me amid work that I cared about, for anyone to think of me as attractive. Best example: My wife and I met in Iraq. She was a journalist covering a delegation I was leading into the Basra region in early 2001. She was attracted to me because she saw me as someone who believed 100 percent in the work that I was doing, and also that I was respected for that work by peers. Worst example: my between-marriage dates described in Chapter 3.

Next we come to the question of "Who are you looking at?" Are you being realistic about who you have a chance with, or are you attracted only to movie star good looks? Just as you may be asking people to see past your inabilities to fit perfectly into mainstream thinking, so too should you reciprocate. We can be unrealistic. We can demand that the world treat us as "one of the guys" yet be judgmental and overly picky with others.

That said, I am for, not against, physical attraction being one of the first indicators of a potential partner, as it is a rare case when two people can make an intimate relationship work when they are not attracted to each other. But mutual interests and an ability to connect (you'll know it when it hits you) should be right up there on your list of priorities.

Jerry Newport, writing in *Your Life Is Not a Label*, suggests another arena to look for someone:

> Heck, why not date a young girl with some other kind of challenge, not necessarily autism? There might be more empathy to share.

If your challenges are significant enough that you live in a supportive housing unit or group home, and you can't work, then the possibility exists that you may not marry, though you can still have intimate relationships. Traditional expectations about marriage involve children, and maybe buying a home together, and it may be difficult for someone else to make the adjustment to married life with someone who is unable to fit into these preconceived notions. But (1) marriage does not *have to* include these traditional expectations, and (2) love is still very possible, even lifelong love.

And for those of you who are not as challenged, your relative inability to "play the game" will be a positive attribute, not a detriment, to a lot of people. You just have to get out there to find such special people, or allow them to find you.

Remember again, regarding failure, that unless you get ridiculously lucky, there will be rejection along the way. But considering all the stress, anxiety, and turmoil that go into asking someone out on a date, you'd be amazed at how much easier it is just to ask. Because when you run from the chance to ask someone out, the lingering regret you'll feel can risk prodding your already vulnerable capacity for low self-esteem.

Dating

In Chapter 3, we went over the pitfalls of the traditional date. Rituals like dinner, dancing, and/or a movie shouldn't be ruled out necessarily, and if you can do well at such traditions, a certain amount of pride should be yours for figuring them out (I couldn't). But if these venues aren't to your liking, GRASP's Zosia Zaks, in *Life and Love: Positive Strategies for Autistic Adults*, has a fabulous list of alternative date ideas, such as the following:

- Go to the library to look something up or to share your favorite books.
- Have a picnic in the park.
- Have a picnic at the garbage dump, so you can watch the trucks smash up the trash.
- Visit a museum, an aquarium, a science center—they often offer free admission days.
- Go hiking at a nature center.
- Take a walk in a neighborhood you've never been to.

Once you're actually on a date, you're somewhat on your own to develop a strategy that is based on the person you're going out with, and what brings the two of you together. But there are some basic rules to follow (especially for those new to dating):

1. Prior to the date, dress appropriately and smell good. Perfumes or colognes aren't necessary (and if the other person is on the spectrum, it might be preferable that you not wear these). But make sure you're clean—teeth brushed, no body odor, etc.

2. At the beginning of the date, say something nice about how your date looks. But don't keep repeating the compliment.

3. Listen to the person you're on a date with. Try not to interrupt.

4. When the topic switches to you, try to be positive. If the subject touches on events in your life that were hard, be honest about them, but don't play them for sympathy. You'll get more respect this way.

5. If the date involves spending money (such as dinner) and you asked the other person out, try to pay, but be prepared to pull back and let the other person contribute if you sense this is somehow insulting to them.

6. At the end of the date, never engage in anything physical unless both of you want to. If you don't want physical contact but want a second date, say "no" nicely so that your wishes are clear.

Numbers 7 through 9 are for those of you who may have challenges that perhaps have prevented you from learning some of the most basic rules. For those to whom these do not apply, it would be helpful to take note should you ever mentor someone with a more severe form of AS . . .

7. Remember that if you are over the age of eighteen and the other person is not over the age of eighteen, you should never, ever engage in sexual activity with that person. You could go to jail for this.

8. Remember to be honest if feelings start to grow. Sometimes people will date more than one person at a time unless there is an agreement between the two to be exclusive.

To be dishonest in this regard is called cheating, and the other person probably won't appreciate it if they find out.

9. If you like someone, he doesn't have to like you back. And if he doesn't like you back, then you have to leave that person alone.

Significant Others: Introduction

It seems possible now to not only reinterpret the past in light of new knowledge and compassion, but to also change the definition of ourselves and our relationship. When this happens to one member of a partnership it must affect the other.

—Aurelia van Hulstey, "Relativity," from the book
Voices from the Spectrum

This diagnosis can also bring good news to a spouse, partner, or long-term boyfriend or girlfriend. For if an individual on the spectrum were to call his spouse's new dress ugly (after his spouse had made it clear to him that she liked the dress), prior to the diagnosis this would have created the appearance of rudeness. It is then usually a very large relief for the spouse to find out that because of the diagnosis, the *intent* to hurt most likely never existed. Furthermore, it can also relieve you—your loved one might not be hurt or angry at you anymore.

Sometimes this isn't the case immediately. And while you can walk away from other family members, if not without pain, it is very hard to do this to a significant other without losing the relationship.

In the cases where the significant other may be too stigmatized by your new diagnosis (for example, your partner is too embarrassed to be with someone on the spectrum), or if your partner blames the diagnosis for everything that has gone wrong in the past, you may have a tough decision to make. Sometimes, the frustration of not knowing that AS was involved in a partnership has, over time, driven both parties into irreparably abusive patterns. In any of these cases, you still have to try. Again, the more you learn about your diagnosis, the more you will learn about your *partner* as well as yourself and why the two of you were drawn together. That information will be helpful to you both in finding ways to make the relationship work, and paradoxically in knowing when it is perhaps time to let the relationship go.

How the Diagnosis Can Affect a Relationship

Together you should try to find the elements of the relationship that have always been *strong* because of your AS. For example, it might have made you:

- more loyal to your partner

- more honest with your partner

- more trustworthy with things such as money

- more willing to give your partner some of her own space

That last bullet has a flip side, however. As Tony Attwood writes in *Asperger's Syndrome*:

> They can avoid any discussion on contentious issues and become socially isolated for hours or days. The person is solving their problems by retreating into their own thoughts, but their partner resents being excluded. They are hurt that at such moments their opinions or ideas are not considered.

In short, you may feel love, you may not still be mad after that last fight, or you may be concerned for your partner at a time of varying crisis; but if you don't communicate these things to him, he will not know that you feel this way. He will simply think you don't care, and logically thinking, he is right to think that. We spectrumites are very much internal creatures regarding emotional issues, partially because sometimes we don't identify the emotions as they happen. It will always be helpful to address the needs of the other person in the way in which *he asks you to*, as opposed to the way you think is best.

Liane Holliday Willey, writing about how she manages married life in *Pretending to Be Normal*, states:

> Like other people make lists to remind themselves to pick up milk or get the mail, I make lists that tell me how to act. On my list are things like—hold Tom's hand for 5 minutes everyday . . . hug Tom 3 times today.

I have heard this very quote criticized for what it supposedly says about her relationship with her husband, that because actions such as holding hands and hugging don't happen automatically, the love is somehow nonexistent. This could not be farther from the truth. Know in your heart that Liane loves her husband very much (which I can admittedly say partly because I know Liane). It's like the boy that Tony Attwood cited in *Asperger's Syndrome*:

> The mother of a teenager expressed her concern that her son with Asperger's Syndrome rarely showed any signs of love for her. He replied that he told her that he loved her when he was six years old and was confused as to why he should have to repeat those words. Surely she knew.

Knowing that feelings exist is different from our capacity to express them in the way others want (and need). Liane simply learned how to *show* her very deeply felt feelings.

Sex

The Aspergerian characteristic of "being too obvious" about our sexual desires can have a silver lining—that most people on the spectrum sexually hear, and act on, their body's impulses. As a result, you will probably not be in danger of failing to communicate what you desire out of your sex life. The challenges may lie with reciprocating, with exhibiting socially appropriate restraint, and the theory of mind notion that your partner might desire a slightly (or perhaps not so slightly) different sex life from what you desire.

Usually, these bodily signals of ours will clearly inform us what level of sexual appetite we all have. Some of us will hear our body's messages that little contact is desired, while others will hear that they desire sexual activity much more than the average person. Both extremes, however, can come with high degrees of anxiety if this appetite level becomes at odds with the differing appetite of a partner.

Education will help. For more active adults who have established relationships, there are many books outlining exercises and exploratory games that you can try out with your partner. These are helpful not only in gently communicating potentially hurtful truths or feelings about an already established sex life, but also in breaking out of sexual routines that have developed within the relationship, routines developed in response to your lives that one or more of you may be dissatisfied with. Yes, you do want someone in your life who has similar likes and dislikes, but you must understand that the desires of both partners can almost never be exactly the same, and you will both have to adapt to that fact, and compromise.

Remember too that every time you have sex with your partner, the mood may be different. Frankly, this is usually preferable as you experience less boredom this way. It may be quiet, sweet, and subdued one day; and then raucous, energetic, fun, or extremely lustful on another. Also, both your bodies will likely be communicating with one another when engaged in sexual activity. You may each be giving off signs to move at different speeds and rhythms, to switch positions, or to experience a similar emotional attachment (or detachment). Consider this to be a form of talking to one another—a form of nonverbal communication that has to be learned, and one that is usually necessary for making the relationship work inside and outside the bedroom.

Lastly, if the books don't work, or if perhaps there is too much anxiety or shame influencing either partner's capacity for making the relationship work, there are sex therapists—psychiatric professionals specialized in this one particular subject. You don't have to tell anyone that you are seeing one (frankly, this isn't advisable except with very close friends), and going through whatever embarrassment this may entail is preferable to an unhappy sex life or, at worst, the relationship ending.

Education will also help those of you who have had little experience. It will teach you how to use birth control, show you the very important definition of what "consent" means, and will help you ward off people who might be trying to trick you (with helpful hints such as never allowing people to pay you for sex, unless you make a conscious decision to become a prostitute).

Alone by Choice

Many people with AS make a conscious choice not to have intimate relationships in their lives. Only they themselves know in their hearts whether this is a true absence of desire, or if anxieties and/or bad histories are playing a larger role. Temple Grandin used to write about having made such a decision long ago, and now in her fifties she has commented in public that she wonders if she made a good decision. But an ability to engage someone in sexual activity, when the very subject terrifies you, will almost always be dependent on finding someone you trust, someone who will still care about you and want to be with you if things don't go as well as they do in the movies. And when you have AS, finding such a trustworthy individual can be difficult.

Much has changed since when Temple made that decision, and I privately hope that she finds someone she too can trust. Admitting some bias in this regard, as someone who enjoys my marriage and who cares about Temple as a legendary maverick— one whose work paved the way for the rest of us with AS—I hope, if the chance arises (and she is too remarkable a person for it not to), that she tries. She is the bravest individual on the spectrum I know (her stories from long ago about when she was the only woman working on ranches are proof). However, the choice is hers, and that of the many GRASP members who have made this decision. And for me or anyone else to attempt to push anyone into sexual or romantic activity (as I have perhaps just done to Temple?) is wrong.

Some people are alone by choice, yes; but some others are alone, sexually desirous, and yet not in a relationship. Quoting Isabelle Hénault from her book *Asperger's Syndrome and Sexuality*:

Some women with AS accept all sexual offers in an attempt to obtain affection and intimate contact, and some people take advantage of their naivety and vulnerability.

A Note About Being Very Sexually Active

Promiscuity is a word that is generally used to describe when a person sleeps with many people. While not a lifestyle that should be entirely discouraged or demonized, promiscuity definitely carries greater danger for women than it does for men. But it still comes with warnings for both genders. Whatever you do now may have an adverse effect on the one you someday fall in love with. For whether right or wrong, the world sometimes wants a partner who doesn't have an extensive sexual history.

1. They may feel threatened by unrealistic (or realistic) ideas that you have had partners who satisfied you more than them.

2. They may fear sexually transmitted diseases such as herpes or the HIV virus.

3. If they are dedicated to certain religions, you may have automatically removed yourself from consideration owing to the laws that they follow (especially if you're a woman).

4. They may wonder if you are too attached to that lifestyle to ever become a trustworthy, monogamous partner who won't cheat on them.

I was lucky. From high school until I was married, I was very active. I never had a long-term relationship because I didn't have a clue how to maintain one. But this was luckily attributed to the idea that I was too focused on my work, rather than on the greater truth that I was clueless as to what was required of me in a long-term relationship. So I got used to the idea of not having one, and I instead engaged in a myriad of short-term relationships. The rewards of a monogamous life, I can honestly say many years later, are infinitely better, but I don't regret the number of partners I had because I truly believe I learned from every one of them. And owing to all the variables that factored into my upbringing, experience was always going to be my best teacher. Furthermore, I was also never dishonest about what others should expect from me regarding possible relationships; so I have nothing to feel guilty about. But I am also a man; there was less at risk both physically and in reputation. Lastly, I was lucky because my first wife trusted that, despite such a history, I had it in me to be faithful. Monogamy for me has not been difficult. In fact, I thrive in it.

Just be careful, and make the smartest choices you can without denying yourself some potentially wonderful experiences.

To sign contracts about what a sexual relationship should entail probably won't become standard practice among new couples anytime soon. Although this crazy idea might appeal to some spectrumites' wishes for no future surprises, it goes against the grain of how the majority of the world operates. However, desires and expectations should always be discussed between partners. For whether sexual encounters are filled with candles, low lighting, and two hours of cuddling afterward, or if they instead last only seconds and are a means for one or both partners to feel relieved of bodily pressure, both partners need to be happy in the relationship. Furthermore, the relationship itself may change one or both partners' feelings about what they desire. Arguably the only connecting emotion that should bind every experience is gratitude, and the aforementioned trust.

ARE we putting too much emphasis on sex? Hénault again, writing in *Asperger's Syndrome and Sexuality*:

> Sexual satisfaction (in terms of sexual frequency and quality) is not necessarily an indication that a couple is happy and fulfilled. However, some neurotypical partners report that their counterparts with AS assume that a satisfying relationship means having an active sexual life.

Lynne Moxon adds to this point in "Diagnosis, Disclosure and Self-Confidence in Sexuality and Relationships," from the book *Coming Out Asperger: Diagnosis, Disclosure, and Self-Confidence*, as she quotes an unnamed Aspie:

> "I want to get married so I don't have to masturbate anymore and I'll have someone to cook for me."

I frankly side more with the individual quoted above than perhaps Hénault or Moxon would approve of. This is someone who at the very least knows, and is communicating, what he wants. Perhaps he is doing so inappropriately, and obviously his understanding of the emotional requirements of a relationship is deeply questionable. But sex *is* important to us. And if people on the spectrum do hold the sexual portion of a relationship as a higher priority than the next person, then it would be completely hypocritical for me, or anyone who regards himself as open to changing attitudes, to try and steer them away from what they want. We should be educated about how to obtain what we want, and how feasible our expectations are, but to be ashamed about our desires is very wrong. So my hope for that person quoted by Moxon is that he finds someone who wants to have sex, and who likes to cook.

Strategies for College

Stephen Shore thought he'd died and gone to heaven when he went to college. For Stephen, he was finally in an environment that cared foremost about his work, and not about "how cool" he was perceived to be. I too enjoyed college, but my last three years of high school were the start of my happiness. Stephen had to wait longer.

Choosing the right college is the first, and most important, strategy. How far away from home do you want to be? Does the school match your abilities well? Are you under- or overestimating your capacity to academically fit in? I, or instance, chose my undergraduate college (Hampshire College) based on three criteria: (1) I thought it was a good school, (2) they allowed pets on campus (again, I was devoted to my dog), and (3) there was a huge emphasis put on independent study outside the classroom so that I wouldn't have to take so many classes. While the noise and social factor would not have made it an ideal school for everyone on the spectrum, I thrived there, and graduated early.

BECAUSE of the greater emphasis on our abilities, many spectrumites will succeed in college. Yet many people on the spectrum have difficulty with both the social and the academic side of college, especially if they haven't mastered independent living skills. The social side of things is more complicated, and much of what will help has been learned in other chapters. Yet just as we go to elementary and secondary schools to learn how to socialize, college can be thought of as years when we're supposed to learn how to live by ourselves.

Still, in combating cruel peer behavior, and/or parties that are usually noisier and more crowded than what you experienced in high school, there are some avenues you can pursue. First and foremost, taking from the beginning of this chapter, establish that environment, starting in your room, that makes you feel good and secure. Holliday Willey suggests two additional ideas that you (1) find other spots on campus that you feel good in (for example, libraries!), and use them; and (2) ask a guidance counselor if there are social groups on campus for students who may be united by a particular interest or hobby. Going further, if one doesn't exist for your interest, you could ask that counselor to help you create one.

As far as your academic challenges are concerned, there are several things you can do. First off, don't overload your schedule. In a noble effort to dive into the rigors of college study, you may be tempted to take on too much. Go easy, perhaps taking the minimum number of classes that won't jeopardize your academic standing or planned graduation date. Second, ask to meet with a professor before signing up for her class. You might want to explain some of your challenges to her in this meeting, not necessarily to ask for special consideration yet, but instead to gauge how receptive she will be to accommodating you *should you ever need her to*. Third, Holliday Willey suggests that if you have any auditory or visual sensory issues, that you find, or ask for, seating where the distractions will be at a minimum.

These different realms of university life (social life and academics) feed off one another. For instance, your social challenges may overwhelm you to the point that they affect your capacity to study. In addition, if you are having difficulty with living by yourself for the first time, this too may affect your performance in class or on campus. If you are having difficulty organizing your daily routine, concoct a schedule for yourself, one that incorporates regular laundry visits, the household or dorm room chores you have, and whatever else adds to your class schedule and academic appointments.

If you have disclosed to your school that you have AS, you may be using their Office of Student Disabilities (with varying wording) or the school's ADA (Americans with Disabilities Act) Compliance Officer. These are federally mandated offices that most schools are required to have on campus for your assistance, and if you had special education accommodations in high school, then you need to continue having them in the new environment. But be warned, many of these offices do very little, existing merely to pay lip service to the law and protect the university from lawsuits. If you need their help, remember that, as in the work world, you must request *specific accommodations*. In other words, you'll have to be the one to think up what will help you. The school is not required to come up with such strategies.

Some classroom accommodations to request might include:

- A person to act as a notetaker (especially if laptop computers are not allowed in class)

- Written instructions to back up any material presented orally by the professor in class

- Permission to use a tape recorder

- Additional time when you are taking both tests and exams

You can also ask for outside class assistance such as review sessions. And if the school is not forthcoming, you could try to create this help if you sense others in the class are having similar difficulties.

Remember too that college won't necessarily prepare you for the social demands of the job you might get, even though they've armed you with the best academic training. If you think you'll need it, try to use your college's resources to find avenues where you can learn about the interview process. Or better yet, try to get them to provide you with social skills workshops. And don't forget to take that ethics class, or a psychology class, an anthropology class . . . all those "how does the rest of the world think" subjects that could help you navigate both campus life and the world outside.

And if you've disclosed your AS and are using the special offices of the university, the least they can do is provide you with an opportunity to meet with, and perhaps create a support group for, all students on campus who are on the autism spectrum. Not only will the "GRASP-ian" sense of shared experience help, but together you might be a much more powerful source for on-campus change if any seems necessary.

Becoming Aware and Getting Involved

When we think of "the politics of the autism world," are we thinking about the following:

- Bills to increase government funding of autism research?

- Legislation that will deny insurance companies the ability to refuse coverage to someone because of her diagnosis?

• Advocating that additional schools be built?

• Advocating for services to be increased?

No. These issues are probably the most important that exist, but they're causes that get universal approval from the entire autism community. They amount to a simple, though difficult fight with government over money.

The problems—the issues that *threaten* the autism community's sense of certainty and unity—lie in four debates:

1. **The word *cure*.** There is no clearer dividing line that measures a person's place in the politics of the autism world than through their reaction to this word. Adults on the spectrum universally seem to dislike the word *cure*. But many researchers, parents, and clinicians find it appropriate, and use it. This is a debate that also has both a medical *and* an ethical component to it.

2. **The vaccine controversy.** This debate concerns whether or not a generation (or generations) of children have become autistic because of tainted childhood immunizations.

3. **The use of "aversives."** To what degree are institutions and schools allowed to potentially hurt people on the spectrum in order to successfully restrain them?

4. **How existing, available money should be spent.** In general, schools and services are subject to state budgets. Outreach and advocacy organizations are privately funded, and so this leaves research as perhaps the only federally funded item. But there are different types of autism research. And currently there is a highly disproportionate amount of money going toward biomedical research (research that

investigates genetic causes, but for what purpose?) as opposed to data-based research that might track how many
people in this country are out of work or need housing.

Many of these debates involve questions discussed in Chapter 1, including:

- whether the autism spectrum is one vastly complex diagnosis, or

- several different diagnoses, or

- whether or not the condition is genetic.

These debates tend to overlap. For instance, if one believes that
autism is genetic, then it couldn't have been caused by vaccines
(though it could have been exacerbated or triggered by them) because you can't *acquire* something that is genetic—you're born
with it and you will die with it. But if autism *isn't* genetic, and if
it is something you "picked up," then it could conceivably be
"cured." Furthermore, if you believe that autism is a horrible diagnosis, and that AS is a separate diagnosis that presents challenges, though not like autism, then you could conceivably wish
for autistics to be cured and AS folk to simply be provided with
better supports. Yet to believe that, you'd have to first find a
proven line in the sand that separates AS and autism.

You are entirely forgiven if you don't care much for these arguments. You have plenty on your plate as it is. But these issues
are worth your investigative time as the knowledge helps to
make sense of *why* the current stigma exists.

Furthermore, you will be indirectly (perhaps directly) affected
by how these debates develop. Once a stranger hears of your diagnosis, his first impression of you will be determined by

preconceived notions, ideas defined by how our society processes what it hears from these debates. Soon after the stranger reacts to this iconography, perhaps the you that is you will change that preconceived notion, no matter how erroneous it is. But participation in these arguments will make that preconceived notion more informed. So contribute, and be a voice. It will make it easier for all of us as we attempt to begin a relationship.

Politics are a necessary evil. But whether we win or lose the "battles," simply waging them brings about changes in perceptions, an aura of accountability from all sides, and the capacity to bravely examine ourselves because we'll be armed with better information. When Stephen Shore presents at conferences or other speaking engagements, he is frequently asked questions afterward about subjects as wide as school IEPs, sensory challenges, and disclosure. But when Stephen first started speaking, the questions often revolved around when he became toilet trained. Our engagement in these controversial issues keeps new insight from becoming buried. We therefore cannot run from these confrontations, even if the emotionally charged nature of them intimidates us. I learned long ago that a cruel fact of leadership is that if you're pleasing 100 percent of the people around you, you probably aren't getting a thing done. The trick lies in *how* one confronts . . .

Temple Grandin, in *Thinking in Pictures: My Life with Autism*, wrote:

> More knowledge makes me act more normal. Many people have commented to me that I act much less autistic now than I did ten years ago . . . The more I learn, the more I realize more and more that how I think and feel is different . . . I think there is too much emphasis on deficits and not enough emphasis on developing abilities.

I've had the same experience. My friend Scott was asking me about AS once, soon after I was diagnosed. He and I had gone to graduate school a dozen years prior, and I was comparing how I now felt with how I felt when we were both studying playwriting together at Columbia. I told him how much easier it now was for me to be myself, now that I finally knew what I had, and that I didn't have to hide my more autistic behaviors anymore. His response was laughter.

"But Michael, you seem so much less autistic now than you did back then . . ."

I see his point. There is less anxiety now—the act of playing a character that wasn't me only added to that past anxiety, a restlessness that currently exists at a fraction of its former level. Knowledge did this.

But knowledge never surfaces without an arena that allows it to circulate truthfully.

Understanding the Difference Between Self-Advocacy and Victimization

When that mother yelled, "But everything he says is so stupid," and members of the Manhattan GRASP meeting rose to stick up for her beleaguered son, my pride wasn't merely reflected in their ability to take such a stand. It was also reflected in their not having gone too far. They shouted her down with facts about the AS mind-set, not with insults.

For the record, *self-advocacy*, by most definitions, is:

- Disclosure, with the added purpose of obtaining supports and/or services

- The ability to tell the world *yourself* about what makes you different, as opposed to needing others to do it for you

- The ability to tell others what accommodations you need (if any) in order to have a relatively happy life

- Having an educated understanding of what you are, and what you are not, entitled to

And as is displayed in the best self-advocates, self-advocacy is also:

- Executing all of the above utilizing social skills in such a way that creates mutual respect between you and the people you are engaged with

My pride in the Manhattan group's instantaneous defense lay in that they did not take their advocacy into that darker, extremist land beyond self-advocacy: victimization.

Victimization, in this context, shouldn't be seen as the penultimate negative that it sounds like, as victimization is often the first feeling of empowerment spectrumites have ever experienced. We can't all transform ourselves instantly into emotionally confident and highly educated reporters regarding our diagnosis, self-advocates who can trust that the world will really hear us. Like everything else, the road from diagnosis to becoming a successful self-advocate is a journey, one that takes time. Victimization can actually be a step toward that promised land. How long the "victim mind-set" lasts, however, will be the measuring stick by which individuals should be judged.

The more negative our experiences prior to diagnosis, the

greater our chances of succumbing to feeling we are victims. Being heard, or trusting that we are being heard, is usually the bridge that is required to become that confident, educated advocate. Victimization, the terrain where we don't yet have that trust, would be a lousy goal to finish at, but it is a far better place to be than when you felt trampled on or remained unaware that those perceptions about you were indeed inaccurate. Heightening our cognitive awareness of how our diagnosis can cause us to be perceived, coupled with seeing the negative consequences of "victimization behaviors," is what will also help to create a self-advocate that can be successful, as opposed to one who only knows how to fight back.

Meeting others on the spectrum is often an enormous confidence builder. After hearing the experiences of fellow spectrumites, you might discover that you have an awful lot to be proud of. You might find that you've handled your diagnosis considerably well overall. And if not, if things have transpired badly for you compared to others, then those whom you meet will probably be your best source for suggestions on how to improve things. Face-to-face support group meetings, despite the sensory and social anxieties they present some of us, are still one of the best sources of such confidence building. Support group meetings give you the chance to hear and share, they validate experiences that others might not believe or understand, and they can also be a safe arena to practice those social skills you might wish to improve.

Should support group meetings not exist in your area, there's always the Internet. Prior to GRASP and other peer-run supports, the Internet was all anyone had. And prior to the Internet, people had the books of Grandin, Williams, and others, but no one to share *back* with. And now there are scads of chat rooms, online communities (GRASP has a Yahoo! group for every regional network), and blogs for people to exchange their feelings and ideas. Often, this is very comfortable territory for the average spectrumite, as in cyberspace:

- The textual nature of the communication renders our challenges at nonverbal communication somewhat moot (our capacity for online discussion has often been compared with the deaf community's use of sign language).

- The textual nature of the communication often reflects a strength toward the written word, one where there is a greater chance at expressing identifiable emotions. Furthermore, such conversations do not require you to sit and stay until you finish them. Unlike a face-to-face conversation, you can take a break if you want or need to.

- The computers needed for implementation are often devices that spectrumites do not fear because of their logic-centered nature.

GRASP has at the very least demonstrated to the clinical world how integral the notion of peer supports is to the well-being of the newly diagnosed person on the spectrum. Such unquestionably successful forums (whether in GRASP's name or through some of the smaller, regionally based groups) will consequently only grow in numbers as the years go by.

Having just spoken about the benefits of the Internet, we should also now look at the pitfalls. Jerry, again, wrote in *Your Life Is Not a Label*:

I've known some people through the Internet and I've met some of them at conferences. Most of them are educated, talented adults who are full of anger. They feel absolutely no obligation to control it. It makes them totally unemployable. They have no control over their lives, but they insist that's the way it has to be and they're perfectly justified in their reasoning. This is a sad waste of a lot of lives.

In addition to the Internet being a place of great exchange and global information, the Internet unfortunately also harbors mean and vindictive people, who often remain under the impression that they can lash out without fear of accountability. The Internet should be explored, tremendously perhaps, but with an understanding, just as in real life, that there are untrustworthy folks mixed in with the trustworthy.

Jane

Hopefully you are beginning to feel more and more empowered by feelings of potential, the eradication of confusion, and perhaps a first-ever sense of shared experience. Yet you might also be prone to feel everyone has to change *except* you. And for anyone, or any organization (such as GRASP), to suggest otherwise might summon defensive instincts.

The real damage that victimization does is not so much to those who get in the way of the "victim"; it's in the opportunities lost by that individual who so believes in his or her persecution.

In early 2007, GRASP was hoping to advocate for a woman on the spectrum who until recently had been attending college in California. She'd been kicked out rather harshly after a series of combative interactions.

On "Jane's" request for advocacy, GRASP explored the situation. We spoke with some of the people involved with what led to her removal from campus, and we had several conversations with the lead counsel from the law firm representing the college. Jane most certainly had a gripe. The college, a school that enjoyed advertising how friendly it was to students with disabilities, had demonized her for behaviors that they completely failed to see were the results of her diagnosis. They'd provided scant evidence documenting the incidents that led to her expulsion, they'd failed to provide her with an entitled appeal hearing regarding the events, they'd thrown her off campus in such a manner that inflicted more trauma than it would a neurotypical, and they'd failed to condemn bigoted remarks made by one particular professor that had set this whole ugly chain of events in motion.

Yet feeling uncertain, and unable to trust, Jane had made no friends in the process. She reportedly was confronting everyone who got in her path—secretaries, receptionists, and others—accusing more than the appropriate personnel of violating her rights. Jane, for the record, was into "rights." She clung to them. Through her passionate absorption in legal matters, she'd learned much about what she was, and was not, entitled to, and I'd surmise that this was her AS at work, pursuing a special interest. But I'd also surmise that she'd gravitated toward this particular field subconsciously to give her a sense of grounding in an uncertain world. Her problem was that, not having a law degree, she'd gotten some things wrong. She was incorrect on certain legal issues and she had great difficulty accepting this. Jane (older than most students) had a history of filing lawsuits on her own, and she was now filing against the school and the offending professor, even though seemingly none of her past suits had resulted in her favor.

I asked Jane what she wanted from GRASP's involvement. She said she wanted to be allowed to go back to school and finish her degree. Going to another school was not in her plans.

In my ensuing conversations with the school's lead counsel,

my point about how they'd mishandled her diagnosis finally seemed to resonate. The lawyer grew to understand that the school, the arguably bigoted professor, and a very vindictive Dean of Student Judicial Affairs had in fact acted as the trigger to almost all of her perceived negative behaviors. So he asked me for a proposal, one that he could submit to the school that would call for GRASP to mediate a solution between the school and Jane. It looked like Jane would be allowed back in. But when I took the good news back to Jane, she was unwilling to bend. She would not relinquish the ability to do things like tape-record phone conversations or accost low-level employees. No mediation would occur.

Being right often isn't what's most important. Understanding what you are and are not entitled to will help enormously, but a defining line in the sand where one crosses over into victimization might very well be when you become a person who knows *nothing other* than what your rights are. Jane thought she was punishing those who had hurt her, yet she was punishing only herself. And despite the very real culpability of this reprehensible college, Jane had filed every offense in perfect detail into her memory banks, where they sat like bad meat in the fridge, paralyzing her ability to forgive, and get a degree.

> I know now that I was just born this way, so I feel I am a "victim" of circumstance. But for all the painful experiences that Asperger's has caused, and I can tell you there have been a lot, there have been many more experiences that were good. And I feel the good greatly outweighs the bad.
>
> —GRASP member Fred Wye

The inflexibility element of autism is a component we, as individuals, must come to terms with. It makes us more loyal in our relationships, more thorough in our work, and more thoughtful in our free time. Yet too often we impose rules that appeal to our fears, and not to our hearts or minds, as we try to accrue that control over situations that we find so desperately foreign. It's the idea that we *can't* control everything that will often make us feel better.

The Best Perspective?

Many of the enlightened younger folks on the spectrum refer to AS as "Wrong Planet Syndrome," and it's a good, fun analogy. But a more realistic, truly workable parallel developed out of a conversation by the Manhattan GRASP Network. These members successfully compared their experiences to those who have gone through the process of coming to this country as an immigrant.

It stands to reason, for most immigrants perform decidedly better in new surroundings if they have neighborhoods to migrate to that contain large pockets of their expatriate countrymen. The shared experience of living in such an enclave provides security and support that turns into strength when the immigrant has to leave that neighborhood to go look for work, or merely navigate life in a brave, new world. Your own language to fall back on, your native songs to sing in the evening, and perhaps a breakfast of your own food in your belly—this great force flooding you as you smile and leave that enclave to try a new food for lunch, or a first phrase or two in that new language. Exploring, learning, blending in, appreciative, but still proud of who you are.

Strategies for . . . ?

We need strategies for far more things in life than just our own self-respect, our families, our work lives, our love lives, and college. Some of us need assistance with driving a car, some with shopping, managing a checkbook, even though others on the spectrum excel in these areas. GRASP member Ruth Snyder couldn't find a church she liked until finally:

> We found peace in one church filled with rocket scientists and engineers.

Ruth's secret was that she kept looking.

Some of us also have children who are on the spectrum. And as is reflected in many areas of AS, there is very little literature available.

My son has never heard a negative word about AS, and I believe he's thrived in these surroundings. He also goes to a good, appropriate school, and his challenges are posed to him in the context of "you can do this if . . ." as opposed to within a concept that states he can't do something. The positive nature of such an approach has him lacking in self-hatred for what neurologically sets him apart. He will endure some unhappy times in later years, no doubt, but everyone involved in his care has prepped him well for how to hopefully overcome such periods.

Having a parent with the same diagnosis can go both ways. It's the parent who doesn't feel less of a person because of the diagnosis who helps immensely toward how the child will view him or herself.

There are also strategies for dealing with obtaining disability benefits, for handling social services coordinators and state agencies—people still relatively ignorant of what AS is despite the fact that they handle people on the spectrum all the time. There are also strategies needed if for any reason you are dealing with something horrible through the court system, though a lawyer should determine what those are. Darius Mc-Collum, for instance, is someone relatively famous with AS, whose fascination with subway and commuter trains, and the inability to stay away from them, has kept him in jail for most of his adult life. Had he ever enjoyed a good lawyer, he probably wouldn't have endured so much incarceration. And this is sad because Darius is a very intelligent, well-spoken, and really nice guy.

Further Resources

The following books, cited repeatedly many times herein, are the best suggested further reading sources for strategies that are out there. These aren't the only great books that exist, but they are books that outline strategies in an appropriately positive light.

Tony Attwood
The Complete Guide to Asperger's Syndrome
London: Jessica Kingsley Publishers, 2006

Liane Holliday Willey
Pretending to Be Normal: Living with Asperger's Syndrome
London: Jessica Kingsley Publishers, 1999

Jerry Newport
Your Life Is Not a Label
Arlington, TX: Future Horizons, Inc., 2001

Stephen Shore, Editor
Ask and Tell: Self-Advocacy and Disclosure for People on the Autism Spectrum
Shawnee Mission, KS: Autism Asperger Publishing Company, 2004

Stephen Shore
Beyond the Wall: Personal Experiences with Autism and Asperger Syndrome
Shawnee Mission, KS: Autism Asperger Publishing Company, 2003

Chantal Sicile-Kira
Autism Spectrum Disorders
New York: Perigee, 2004

Zosia Zaks
Life and Love: Positive Strategies for Autistic Adults
Shawnee Mission, KS: Autism Asperger Publishing Company, 2006

FOR STRATEGIES IN EMPLOYMENT ONLY
Temple Grandin and Kate Duffy
Developing Talents: Careers for Individuals with Asperger Syndrome and High-Functioning Autism
Shawnee Mission, KS: Autism Asperger Publishing Company, 2004

Roger N. Meyer
Asperger Syndrome Employment Workbook: *An Employment Workbook for Adults with Asperger Syndrome*
London: Jessica Kingsley Publishers, 2001

FOR STRATEGIES WITH SEXUALITY ONLY
Isabelle Hénault
Asperger's Syndrome and Sexuality: *From Adolescence Through Adulthood*
London: Jessica Kingsley Publishers, 2005

Wendy Lawson
Sex, Sexuality and the Autism Spectrum
London: Jessica Kingsley Publishers, 2005

One More Strategy: Travel

Everything compiled in this chapter has been assembled, processed, and filtered either from books written by far better "strategists" than I, or from the multitude of stories I've heard from our GRASP members. The one original contribution I can offer this chapter has had surprisingly little written about it, the strategy of travel.

When I was in high school, someone once made fun of me with a remark that I did not realize was meant as an insult. The person said, "Act like you belong," and I cluelessly took this as constructive help. "Oh yeahhh," I thought to myself. "That's it! I don't have to belong, or feel sameness. I just have to *pretend* that I do!" Whatever the intention of the advisor, the fact is, the phrase worked.

Travel, as a means of gaining confidence, can be experienced anywhere along the spectrum. When GRASP was helping the New York City Public Schools' Special Education District design a summer program,* travel training was a must. Students' eyes lit up as they figured out how to ride a bus or take the subway for the first time. It wasn't even so much the accomplishment of the day that lifted them; they also smelled what the future could hold. They sensed how wonderful it might be to go to unknown territories all by themselves: to taste those new foods, to meet new people, and to be on their own clock about when it was okay to sit against a wall for five minutes, when it was okay to spend some pocket money, or when it was time to start heading back home. All the kids, you see, were used to being on someone else's clock when traveling. Even caregivers who ask, "Do you want to sit against a wall for five minutes?" say this kindly *on their time*. In these cases, the person on the spectrum must wait to have the opportunity offered to them.

My family pushed travel on me. The excess money in our house was never spent on gadgets or luxuries when I was growing up. Instead, there were trips—lots of them—that my mother had saved for, including the summers of 1969 and 1971, when my mother threw me and a lot of camping equipment into the car and hit the road. Or the trips that took place during two summers when I was eleven and thirteen, when my grandparents rented out a house by a pistachio farm on a small Greek island (Aegena), travels where I would learn that making a pass at a girl in another country can get you thrown into the sea by her brothers.

I was a good student for my family. After graduating from

* The "RSVP," Recreational, Social, and Vocational Program, which in 2007 finished its third successful summer.

college and before I would start graduate school in New York City that fall, I spent three months in Eastern Europe in 1986. I studied a little at the Bertolt Brecht Archives in East Berlin, but I spent most of the time bumming around Poland, Czechoslovakia, and Hungary, as well as other parts of East Germany.* I played with fire, dodged the police on several occasions (nothing too criminal; I just didn't comply with any of their registration, curfew, and housing requirements), and had the time of my life. I heard from people with perspectives that were so new to me, and they in turn didn't seem to find me so weird. And it quickly dawned on me that travel was very much about having a clean slate. You were with people who didn't know you, who didn't know any negative histories or the reputations for weirdness you might have accrued. Far too many people on the spectrum spend most of their days with people who carry around memories of, and are often too overwhelmed by incidents of, prior misinterpretation. This is no fun. In travel you can start over, and reinvent yourself. If somehow a relationship gets weird, you can leave and go to the next town, the next block, or whatever the case may be, and try again.

Two years later, in 1988, after most of my graduate classes were finished at Columbia, my advisors pushed for me to go on another trip. They wanted me to go pretend to be an eighth-rate Jack Kerouac for my thesis. The plan was that I work odd jobs to pay for food and gas as I traveled across the United States, and then return for the fall semester, and so I did—sort of. I lived out of my car for four months, not two, and nearly never came back. Had I not returned, I would have been making a

---

* Traveling in other countries is especially fun because others often attribute your differences to the less-stigmatizing idea that you're like this only because you're a foreigner.

massive mistake, but I felt as self-sufficient as I ever will. I felt I could find work wherever I was, my expenses were very low, and I was truly enjoying myself. Such true independence is very seductive.

On this trip, I played with fire even more, for the best guarantee of an adventure was to walk into a small town, find a local bar, put two quarters down on the pool table, and start drinking (stories for a future book perhaps). There was foolishness, stupidity, and great risk. But my advisors knew more than I. They sensed my feeling ostracized, and they sensed that my interest in other cultures might cause me to move to another country, which they didn't want. They were right, as moving to Europe was secretly my plan. And they were further right in that, owing to that trip, I was finally made to feel welcome in my own home. Therein too was a clean slate everywhere I went. And as the trip wore on, and I developed vocal inflections, and wore clothes that by trial and error made me more likable to the people I came across, my confidence soared as it never had before. Not because I always want to pretend to be something I'm not, but because I could indeed acclimate myself if I wanted to.

Shortly before my son C.C. and I went on a hiking trip to Utah in 2004, there was an emergency phone call. One twenty-three-year-old man with AS whom GRASP had worked with had experienced a breakdown. "Harry," whom I've written about elsewhere before, was one of those few who just wanted to wake up one morning and find out that he never had AS, that it was all just a bad dream. One night the family came home to find Harry's shoes in the house, yet Harry and his bicycle were gone. Eventually, the police found him, barefoot, collapsed from exhaustion beside his bike on the entrance ramp to a state highway. The family had him hospitalized.

"Harry, I don't want to do this. But I need to know you're

safe," his mother said from a chair beside his bed in the emergency room, in her own way trying to hide a question as a statement. "It's okay, Mom," Harry said. "I understand. I just felt that if I kept pedaling, I'd be free."

One night, after C.C. was asleep in our Utah motel beside a mountain range, I stepped outside and just looked up. Nearby peaks were lit by the moon; and for an unprofessional moment I privately wished Harry could have made it out there on his bike, and joined us. All Harry wanted was independence.

CHAPTER SIX

Special Interests = Passion (+ Future?)

It seems that for success in science or art, a dash of autism is essential. For success, the necessary ingredient may be an ability to turn away from the everyday world, from the simply practical, an ability to re-think a subject with originality so as to create in new untrodden ways, with all abilities canalized into the one specialty.
—Hans Asperger, from his doctoral thesis of 1944

From Chapter 1 . . .

Characteristic	Negative Interpretation	Positive Interpretation
Intense absorption in a topic or field of interest.	Individual is obsessed, and is driven further into this absorption by anxiety and stress.	Individual is passionate about a topic or field of interest.

Chances are you once gave enormous amounts of energy to special interests. Chances are you once loved your subject dearly, whether it was trains, animals, or number theory. Chances are your interests changed over time—but your level of commitment did not. It was probably always high. Chances are you were passionate.

Chances are also that these passions were sometimes discouraged. Perhaps people were frightened by your exclusion of other subjects, your exclusion of peers, or your inability to focus on mandated responsibilities. Perhaps such absorption simply scared people, causing them to mistake your passion for obsession. Or perhaps they were simply frightened by a level of engagement that they themselves would never know in their lives. After all, we all fear the unknown.

A high percentage of you experienced extreme difficulty concentrating on subjects that did not interest you. On those occasions you tried, it may have felt like someone was tearing your head apart. Hopefully, however, there were other times in your childhood, when burying yourself in the work that you loved brought affirmation from those around you. Perhaps as you accrued knowledge (and ordered it according to your needs so as to remember it better), there was a pat on the back, an A+from a teacher, or a simple "wow" from an onlooker.

Perhaps you were often lost in thought, and to an infinitely more hallucinatory degree than most folks experience.

We have a very interesting inner thoughtscape and can daydream for ages. My associative thought processes lead me to ideas and possibilities much more interesting than the subjects taught in school.

—Clare Sainsbury, *Martian in the Playground*

And the price of such dedication was perhaps an inability to pay attention to, or care about, the latest fads, the latest clothes, the favored sports teams, peers, or even the expectations of loved ones.

Because your passion didn't resonate as it "should have" in society's still-limited collective thinking of what passion should look like, people might have tried to steer you away from either these interests or the amount of time you spent on them. You perhaps didn't look like Luciano Pavarotti when he sang in an operatic love duet, and perhaps you didn't look like the hockey star Alexander Ovechkin going after a loose puck. Your emotions were displayed differently, and so people didn't see them.

Is such involvement always a positive? No. When my son C.C. was four, he followed the trail of a stream from one end of the Brooklyn Botanical Gardens to the other. It eventually grew into an obligation every time we went. What had once been a calming experience had been mastered, and he had no next level to take his interest to. This frustrated him, and it meant that he needed a new special interest to devote his attention to, or a new and more challenging body of water to follow. The affection he was giving his beloved stream suddenly wasn't reciprocated.

The stresses of socialization and sensory issues probably drive us into that need for routine, for control, and so we find controllable routines that appeal to us. But whatever the origin of our ability to "dive," be it out of choice or necessity, this desire to bury yourself in work that you love, this heightened commitment level to your chosen activities and subjects, should never end. Even if the perfectionist portion of this part of you might require adapted flexibility, go back to that part of you; or if it never left, take greater heart and thankfulness for its presence in your life.

THE abilities you showed might very well deviate from others on the spectrum.

> Visual thinkers, like me, think in photographically specific im-
> ages . . . Music and math thinkers think in patterns. These people
> often excel at math, chess, and computer programming . . . Ver-
> bal logic thinkers think in word details. They often love history,
> foreign languages, weather statistics, and stock market reports.
> —Temple Grandin, *Thinking in Pictures: My Life with Autism*

And what you love might not always reflect that which you're
naturally gifted at. As Donna Williams writes in *The Jumbled
Jigsaw*:

> There are blind people who have flown planes, deaf musicians,
> and paraplegics who have climbed mountains.

Elijah Wapner, the teen son of GRASP Board member Valerie
Paradiz, who was recently featured on an MTV special, is defy-
ing everything we assume about what abilities we have an inside
track to, and those that we don't. He is passionately pursuing a
career as a stand-up comic. And God forbid, partly because he
works his butt off at it, this young man is really funny.

> Life is not meant to be lived indifferently. Given a choice between
> a passion—a genuine interest—and a skill that's dumped in my
> lamp, I'll take the passion any day.
> —Jerry Newport, *Your Life Is Not a Label*

Older readers should not fall victim to that myth about old dogs
and new tricks. We always have the capacity to learn. The happi-
est retirees always seem to be the ones who have delved into
learning things they never had the time for prior. They experience a renaissance, whereas other seniors either bide their time,
or attempt to recover from unmet expectations.

Dr. Temple Grandin isn't thought of as the living pinnacle of autistic possibility merely because her communicative abilities have grown so much over the years, nor is she upheld in such a way only because she writes such successful books. Dr. Grandin turned her early fascinations toward livestock into a career wherein she revolutionized the entire meat industry, designing infinitely more humane and productive cattle-processing facilities.

The laws of probability teach us that we probably won't reach her heights, the heights of an Albert Einstein, an Emily Dickinson, or a Glenn Gould. I couldn't make it as a playwright despite ability, love, and twelve years of supreme dedication. But I'm a better person for having tried, and the level of commitment I've attempted to give to everything I do has translated into pride, and enough successes elsewhere so that I feel fulfilled.

And considering what you now know about your place in society, there may be an added incentive. For GRASP member Kevin Simonson:

> I made the difficult decision to go back to graduate school and pursue my Ph.D. . . . . I felt like I owed it to people on the autistic spectrum everywhere to show what someone else on that spectrum could accomplish.

Silence

Are you discouraged by what you've read? Are you convinced, for whatever reason, that such immersion is impossible? Then let me try to convey yet another "strategy": Trust silence. In silence, this ability to focus begins.

Whether it's our AS, accumulated anxieties, or stress, chances are that there are more thoughts racing around our heads at a given moment than exist in the next person. Even when we know that we need occasional "chill" time, those racing thoughts can often feel like they are all that is truly ours. Despite how overwhelming they might occasionally feel, we don't want to lose them, and so true silence can be a scarier proposition than one might think.

When I was young, my mother and I frequently visited her parents' home for family dinners. Joined by her brother and his family, there were eight of us at the table. I was lucky, in that my family fostered unquestionable love and loyalty. But we made for a particularly "yappy" gathering, myself included, and these Sunday conversations often did not go well. Topics would end with someone feeling insulted. Or prior to concluding, the conversations would hit peaks of surprising pettiness and inflexibility. People got hurt far more than they needed to. But one of us was the exception: my maternal grandfather. A respected and somewhat feared patriarch, he sat at the end of the table biding his time, choosing his limited words, as well as the timing of these words, so as to maximize their effectiveness. Feeling somewhere inside me that my out-of-control talking was more unpleasant than pleasant, I was always relieved to be seated next to him. I trusted his ability *and* his methods in holding me accountable.

When I was old enough to help him with firewood, he would occasionally take me with him into the woods, and with the simplest of direction I was informed that our work—cutting and pulling down trees, sawing, splitting, hauling—was to be conducted in near silence. Conversations after the work was done seemed fine by him. But beforehand, his favor could be won by my stopping those thousands of ideas in my head, or the words that wished to follow out of my mouth. At first, this premeditated routine, and the silence, was terrifying. "Have I angered him? . . . And if these thoughts leave me, what will I have left?" But soon I noticed how zeroed in I was on the wood, and not my competing thoughts. My grandfather knew exactly what he was doing. Soon I was at peace, and in love with the mind-cleansing labor I had just discovered. Herein I found my capacity to focus, and it was as liberating a lesson as I had ever known. Manual labor jobs followed all through my school years, starting when I was twelve, not simply because the extra money provided greater independence, but also because I now knew what a great effect such soothing effort could have on the rest of my day.

When C.C. was four, he had no interest in sports. I was fine with this. But my concern was that if he should later wish to engage in the same sports his peers participated in—even if it was only socialization that motivated him—he would not be able to play with them if he didn't have certain basic skills at catching and throwing. But when I would take C.C. to the park with a variety of balls, he would talk, and talk—about how we could change the game, or about how bored he was. Even at such a young age he knew how great his power was at discourse, his capacity for textual manipulation, at using words to deflect attention as well as direct it.

So we developed a routine: Once a week we would spend an hour playing what I termed *silent catch*. During this hour there was absolutely no talking allowed. He could choose between a football, a baseball, a Frisbee, or a big rubber ball, but there could be no interruption. In the silence C.C. was eventually able to let go of his thoughts, and just start to Zen in on the rhythms of the exchange. We did this for two years.

At first he was reluctant. But eventually his focus became more zeroed in on the ball, and the repetitive action provided him with a sense of rhythm that kept prior feelings of distracting imbalance from taking over his mind. He accrued the skills, ironed out some motor issues, and the hour passed by quicker and quicker.

THERE are more challenges than gifts, perhaps, inherent in a diagnosis of AS. But there are potential gifts, and the ability to bury yourself in deep interests and passions is the greatest one we so far know of. Cultivate this; it is a gift to yourself, and to others.

CHAPTER SEVEN

Happiness

And this our life, exempt from public haunt,
Finds tongues in trees, books in the running brooks,
Sermons in stones, and good in everything.
—William Shakespeare, *As You Like It*, Act II, Scene 1

IT's now a fairly well-documented, comic/tragic fact that winning the Lotto doesn't bring about happiness. Such an unexpected infusion of money, long thought to be a remedy for all of life's ills, has been widely reported to have split families apart more so than it has brought them together. Whether through financial mismanagement, confusion, a loss of identity, or unmet expectations of fulfillment, the allure of giant jackpots has been tainted by the continuing and growing stories of winners whose dreams didn't end up as they'd planned.

And on the other end of the "fortune versus misfortune spectrum," let's look at those who live through a crippling injury, the sudden death of a loved one (perhaps loved *ones*), or a multiplied combination of these misfortunes brought about by catastrophic events of natural or man-made origin. It's a less-documented fact that people who experience such tragedy can still recapture the happiness they once knew prior, if they were indeed once happy.

Knowing what happiness feels like seems to provide those who endure unfortunate events with an eventual pathway out of their perceived bad fortune.

Love helps, purpose helps, and *our attitudes toward our lives* seem to play a far bigger role than the events in our lives themselves. Yet after that there is no real definition of happiness that I would dare to make. A "happiness" chapter exists herein not because I know what it is, but instead for these two reasons:

1. The most distressing thing I have noticed, from all the stories I have heard from fellow spectrumites, is that happiness is more of a new idea to all of us than we might dare imagine. Somewhere deeply embedded in most spectrumites is a festering notion that traditional (or sometimes even nontraditional) notions of happiness will always be outside our reach.

2. In prior careers I was content just being thought of as good at what I did. I termed this *happiness*. But now knowing so much more—in fatherhood, in reciprocated love—I am astonished by how little I knew prior, and I still hear a little voice that resentfully asks if I deserve to be happy.

Whether happiness is the elusive abstract of number one, or a misinformed description as outlined in number two, the resentful voice is what alarms me. And I fight this wrongful, unnecessary, and misplaced guilt with daily thankfulness, a gratitude to whatever it is that has caused me to be so blessed. And perhaps hypocritically throwing my beloved pluralism in the trash can, I want others to experience these wonderful feelings. Choosing to be unhappy should not be an option.

All the good news contained in this diagnosis is "good" only toward the goal of making you happy. Happiness for the person with AS, perhaps obtainable, perhaps not, is your *right* just as much as it is for anyone else. And as you question how you yourself define happiness, don't be fooled, and don't set your standards low: Determination, compromise, and contentment are not the same as happiness.

When I wrote GRASP members to ask for what their definition of happiness was, many wrote back that it was something close to the alleviation of stress, or a reduction in feelings of uncertainty about the world.

> People are happy when they are in control.
>
> —Bryce R. Howe

> Contentment. And a low-stress environment.
>
> —Gregory H. Gorski

The stress-free definition, as identified by other contributors, also encompassed issues of diet and exercise, alleviating sensory assaults, learning to hug, and finding the right medications to ward off these anxieties. True, such elements would provide immense relief or reduce depression. But is relief the same as happiness? And aren't such contributions more about what we want, but don't yet have? Isn't this an imagined rather than realized happiness?

Others, however, did not picture happiness as a reduction in anxiety. Others wrote about happiness as the joy one feels when the diagnosis appears like a knight in shining armor to destroy all prior confusions and feelings of blame—the whole notion of coming to terms with who you are as opposed to who you aren't.

For some, happiness was defined by career success. This was once how I judged happiness and so I know this definition well. Even now, running GRASP, I am provided incredible satisfaction as I watch the sense of progress people on the spectrum are having as they demand a voice in how they are referred to and treated. Couldn't I term this happiness? Doesn't this count?

Perhaps AS will someday mean nothing in the grand scheme of things—people with neurological and behavioral differences, like those with different skin color or religion, will one day be included into society with the same opportunities and undeniable rights as anyone else. It's a long way off, but I see that day, a day when GRASP is no longer needed. And this is so beautifully good because the ultimate goal of any nonprofit (such as GRASP) should always be its own abolition.

Is happiness such acceptance, is it just positive supports, independence, or is it exclusively just the mountain-moving power of being in love?

Whatever the case, it must be realized, and not imagined. And it must come from our own definitions, as well as those conveyed by conventional thinking.

We often expect an Autie to behave as though a multi-track world is ideal, enjoyable, appreciated and desired. We often expect an Autie to behave as though they have the same intellectual or interpretive interests as anyone else, even if they struggle extremely with receptive information processing and live in a world of pattern, theme and feel in which information is processed well after the event, often pre-consciously.

—Donna Williams, *The Jumbled Jigsaw*

My words are intended to help you live in a world that is populated by people who aren't like you. Because they are the majority, they assume that the only way you can be happy is to be like them.

—Jerry Newport, *Your Life Is Not a Label*

And yet we are not all immune to the happiness others experience when they dress well, or are athletically gifted. Sometimes it is seeing the same sunset that others see that makes us happy. And at other times there is the happiness in having some AS-influenced insight into that sunset, a perspective that sets your appreciation of it apart.

> Nobody can say you can't do it. You will compete with the rest of them, albeit with some modifications because there are some things you know you will never be able to do as well as the rest of them. But you will stay in the game. You are determined to make something of your life, to find some value in it, to keep trying, to keep getting back up and trying different things, no one can say you can't participate, no one can say you're too disabled to do anything, you will show them, but in the back of your mind, at night, during the day, sometimes during every free moment of a bad day, you wonder if they are right. You wonder if perhaps after all you can't do it, you can't do the things you dreamed of, you can't participate in the world, maybe it's just too hard, what if they're right, what if your thoughts are right, what if, what if. What if it gets worse . . .
>
> —Kate Goldfield, GRASP Advisory Board member

That absence of anxiety and stress again . . . while it may not be happiness, it does seem attributable to minor miracles.

———————

THE world of Asperger's syndrome, autism, even all disabilities in general . . . it reflects larger things. It is extremely hard for us all to look upon another who has less (less strength, fewer material things) and believe that this other could be happy. And perhaps we subliminally submit to these misperceptions in order to fit in. Perhaps these are Darwinian survival instincts at work, and perhaps this is about our collective inability to look at human frailty of any kind without being scared, perhaps scared of confronting our own frailty, perhaps scared of our own mortality. Perhaps such instincts and reactions help us to avoid facing the corruption we suffer when we collectively fail to accommodate those who are more vulnerable than we—those around us who are in need—when as the richest society on earth, we easily could.

Now you know. And there is no need to skip to any fantasized future world filled with behavioral pluralism, to see that just because you have an autism spectrum diagnosis you are not excused from the obligation of trying to be a good person—from suffering, from being brave, from experiencing rejection and acceptance, from feeling for someone who has less than you, and from being happy, even if that happiness comes at a definition that may not coincide with the definitions presented to you by the neurotypical world. These are rights, yes, but they are also responsibilities, responsibilities toward responsibility itself that do not fight against the goals of personal happiness; they contribute to them. As Antoine de Saint-Exupéry once said, "The meaning of life isn't found. It is built."

Looking Back, Looking Ahead

When I asked my son what fictional name he wanted me to use in place of his own for this book, he chose "C.C." after the baseball pitcher C.C. Sabathia. Two years ago, Little League was the first non-"special" peer-socialization program that he'd ever participated in. On a team with a lot of older kids, he did his time on the bench, his social connections went okay (nothing stellar, but he wasn't ostracized by any means), and he learned a lot. Last year he wanted to pitch, partially because he'd worked very hard at it; and I told him he wasn't ready. But the head coach disagreed. And I couldn't have been more wrong. Over the course of the season the head coach gave out only three game balls: C.C. got two of them, and the coach called C.C. one of the best pitchers in the league.

When C.C. and I play catch, we get a rhythm going, a rhythm between two people, until it becomes an unconscious act. Once the pattern is established, we can then start to mix things up a little; and in the clearest form of nonverbal communication, C.C. tells me through a throw with some zip on it, that he's ready for one *back* with a little zip. This is an addictive exercise, seducing you with its ideas that you get something back for everything you put into it. There's an underlying sense of justice to it, and the addictive quality emerges because in our love lives and work lives we do not often get an equal return on our investments. But as you do in catch, you do in fatherhood. You do the time, you get a return. Now he throws a pop fly, wanting one back; then a grounder, and so on. It lulls you into a deep trance.

The inherent purpose I have always felt as the head of GRASP has made writing this book easy. What was difficult was the surprise with which I discovered that things for me were harder than I'd ever wanted to admit. Not only did I rely heavily on the idea of just "pressing on" but I too am a victim of the aforementioned Cowboy Culture, one that tried to convince me that in honestly examining my own difficulties, I'd therein be throwing myself a sickening pity party, and perhaps stall my journey. That "culture," like my prior reluctance to fess up, was the real cowardice. C.C., Kathryn, and C.C.'s new baby brother have had to deal with these feelings over the past months, and shoulder me, but now it's baseball season again . . .

Feeling supported, engaging in passionate interests, and being happy matter more than functionality levels, and that's maybe the best lesson to be derived from this book.

It's also a lesson I can prove . . .

When C.C. and I were diagnosed, I didn't yet know the potential harm of the term *high-functioning*, so it was inevitable that we all looked at the question of:

Who's more high-functioning—you or C.C.?

The answer at the time was me. C.C. clearly showed a slightly more challenged brand of AS than what people figured or remembered I'd had.

And yet now?

Soon to be eleven, C.C. is emotionally and developmentally light-years ahead of the eleven-year-old I once was. He has great supports, he knows about his AS, and good people are working very hard to alleviate decades of negative iconography surrounding his differences. We are *all* playing C.C.'s cards better.

C.C. is the new world, living evidence of change. He will have challenges of his own, most certainly, experiences that are incomparable to mine. His walk will be different, but he will have to walk it. And as I play catch with him, and see him receiving my harder throws with a smile, freed by an awareness of himself that I and so many others have only now received, I marvel at him. I feel his strength. His forty-two-year-old father's still-influential ways will resonate less and less as C.C.'s world takes shape.

It's getting late, but we keep playing. He looks like he's going to have a great season.

Call it the long-since-healed wounds of my own fatherlessness; call it coming from parents who loved me unconditionally; call it happiness, pride, love, or just the hypnotic promise of spring. But I could do this forever.

Appendix

About GRASP

GRASP, the Global and Regional Asperger Syndrome Partnership, is the largest educational and advocacy organization in the world serving adults who are diagnosed along the autism spectrum. Other than its proven support networks, its educational outreach, and its role as an informational clearinghouse on autism-related issues, what separates GRASP are the stipulations GRASP must adhere to in accordance with its bylaws—that the Executive Director, 100 percent of the Advisory Board, and 50 percent of the Board of Directors of GRASP must all be diagnosed along the autism spectrum.

While its peer-run nature is key to its existence and provides much of its authority, GRASP is not an isolationist organization. GRASP has many professional affiliations and works in tandem with parent organizations, universities, schools, service agencies, research institutions, larger autism organizations, and other advocacy organizations. That said, its mainstays are those growing numbers of regional support groups run by people on the spectrum. These provide not only the therapeutic quality of shared experience, but also the informational means for self-advocacy and enlightenment to take place in people's lives.

For more information about GRASP, please go to their website at www.grasp.org. There, you can subscribe to one of their many networks and listservs, or just download months of reading from their "articles" page. All subscriptions and support groups are free.

Now that you've heard what GRASP does, I would be a terrible Executive Director if this section did not begin with an appeal . . .

GRASP can be seen in two views. On one hand, we skyrocketed in a very brief period into the largest organization of adults diagnosed along the autism spectrum in the world. Through our growing number of regional support networks, our daily subscriber additions, and through the outreach of our many messages of acceptance and accommodation, we expanded at a rate that was beyond even *our* wildest dreams. But compared with how large this country (or this world) is, compared to the budgets of larger autism organizations, we are still a small, startup nonprofit. Yet we someday hope to be the autism spectrum's version of the National Association for the Advancement of Colored People (NAACP), the Arab American Institute, or the Jewish Defense League. To do that, we need funds, both to sustain such growth as well as to grow further.

If you are an adult who has benefited from our free subscriptions or groups, and who has the means, please give so that others can enjoy the same boost in self-esteem and empowerment that you enjoyed.

If you are a parent, GRASP was the first (and is still currently) the only autism organization to focus primarily on adults. And if you want your children to enter a world that accepts them for who they are, as opposed to who they are not, then I hope you will help GRASP to continue to spread its message.

If you are a friend of someone on the spectrum, give because you know that peer-run supports will foster independence and self-respect. And if you simply agree with GRASP's platform, whether it is our belief in the joy of shared experience, the pride in self-advocacy, or in the purpose of anticure sentiments and the behavioral pluralism that is perhaps the new arena of civil rights, please help. Our budget is barely six figures this year. Given our success rate, think of what we could do with the budgets of larger organizations.

Thank you for listening. If you are able and willing to help, please write a check made out to "GRASP" and mail it to our offices at 666 Broadway, Suite 830, New York, NY 10012; or make a secure PayPal donation by credit card through our website at www.grasp.org/donate.htm. Or you can help us by raising money and/or by spreading our mission in your local community. GRASP is a 501(c)3 tax-exempt organization. And we promise to put your gifts to good use.

Resources

For a current list of available GRASP support groups, please visit www.grasp.org/res_sg.htm.

Other Peer-Run Adult Supports

There are some regional peer-run groups that are not affiliated with GRASP. But I wouldn't include them if they weren't run by good folks. They are:

In San Francisco: Autastics, www.autastics.org.

In Washington, DC: The Asperger Adults of Greater Washington, www.aagw.net.

For highly active adult online message boards, you can go to www.wrongplanet.net or www.aspiesforfreedom.com.

For an annual retreat called "Autreat" (usually held in June) wherein all stims and behavioral differences are encouraged, you can visit Autism Network International's website at http://ani.autistics.org.

For Families

Before getting to supports, there are four wonderful books for parents available. They're not the only great ones either, but they're the "must-reads."

Valerie Paradiz
Elijah's Cup: A Family's Journey into the Community and Culture of High-Functioning Autism and Asperger's Syndrome
London: Jessica Kingsley Publishing, 2005

Clare Sainsbury
Martian in the Playground
Bristol, UK: Lucky Duck Publishing, 2000

Chantal Sicile-Kira
Adolescents on the Autism Spectrum: A Parent's Guide to the Cognitive, Social, Physical, and Transition Needs of Teenagers with Autism Spectrum Disorders
New York: Perigee, 2006

Chantal Sicile-Kira
Autism Spectrum Disorders: The Complete Guide to Understanding Autism, Asperger's Syndrome, Pervasive Developmental Disorder, and Other ASDs
New York: Perigee, 2004

For parents and families (as well as often for adults), there are wonderful resources for both information and support groups available. On a national level, there are the following:

The Autism Society of America www.autism-society.org/site/pageserver

MAAP Services for Autism www.maapservices.org

Regional Groups

On the regional level, there are a multitude of great networks.
In the New York City Tri-State (including Connecticut and New Jersey) Area, there are the following:

The Asperger Syndrome and High-Function Autism Association (primarily NYC and Long Island), www.ahany.org

The Asperger Syndrome Education Network (primarily New Jersey), www.aspennj.org

The Connecticut Autism Spectrum Resource Center, www.ct-asrc.org

New York Families of Autistic Children, www.nyfac.org

Other regional groups include the following:

In the San Francisco area: AASCEND, the Autism and Asperger Syndrome Coalition for Education, Networking, and Development, www.aascend.net/index.shtml

In the Philadelphia area: ASCEND, the Asperger Syndrome Alliance for Greater Philadelphia, www.ascendgroup.org

Index

About the Authors

Michael John Carley received his B.A. from Hampshire College in 1986 and his M.F.A. from Columbia University in 1989. As the Executive Director of GRASP, the largest organization comprised of adults on the autism spectrum, he has spoken at conferences, hospitals, universities, and health care organizations. He has appeared in the media widely, most notably in the *New York Times*, *Washington Post*, *NY Newsday*, *London Times*, *Chronicle of Philanthropy*, *Chronicle of Higher Education*, *Newsweek OnAir*, *Psychology Today*, on Terry Gross's *Fresh Air*, and on NPR's *The Infinite Mind*. NPR news also aired a twelve-minute news piece that featured him and GRASP in June 2006. Carley was featured in the documentary *On the Spectrum* and in the soon-to-be released documentary *Neurotypical: The Movie*. His articles have been published in magazines such as *Autism Spectrum Quarterly*, *TAP (The Autism Perspective)*, *Autism/Asperger Digest*, and in newsletters such as *The OARacle*.

Until 2001, Carley was the United Nations Representative of Veterans for Peace, Inc. In that time, he was known primarily for his work in Bosnia, and in Iraq as the Project Director of the internationally acclaimed Iraq Water Project. Prior to 2001 he was a playwright who enjoyed fifteen productions and ten readings of his plays in New York. Today, in addition to running GRASP, he moonlights as a backup classical music host for New York Public Radio (WNYC). Along with his (then) four-year-old son, he was diagnosed with AS in November 2000. He lives with his wife, Kathryn Herzog, and two sons in Brooklyn. This is his first book.

Peter F. Gerhardt, Ed.D., is President of the Organization for Autism Research, a nonprofit organization, the mission of which is to fund applied research and disseminate the relevant findings in support of learners with autism spectrum disorders and their families. Dr. Gerhardt has over twenty-five years of experience utilizing the principles of applied behavior analysis (ABA) in support of adolescents and adults with autism spectrum disorders in educational, employment, and community-based settings. He is the author or coauthor of numerous articles and book chapters on the needs of adults with autism spectrum disorder, the school-to-work-transition process, assessment of social competence, and analysis and intervention of problematic behavior. He has presented nationally and internationally on these topics. Dr. Gerhardt received his doctorate from the Rutgers University Graduate School of Education.

Dr. Gerhardt has been an active member of Maryland ABA since relocating to Maryland (from New Jersey) six years ago. Previously, he had served on the Board of Directors of New York State ABA and was a founding director of Connecticut ABA. Dr. Gerhardt was recently awarded the John W. Jacobson Award for Significant Contributions to Effective Behavior Intervention by New York State ABA.